D0044366

THE
HUNGOVER
COOKBOOK

THE
HUNGOVER
COOKBOOK

Milton Crawford

Clarkson Potter/Publishers
New York

Published in the United States by Clarkson Potter/Publishers,
an imprint of the Crown Publishing Group, a division of
Random House, Inc., New York.
www.crownpublishing.com
www.clarksonpotter.com

CLARKSON POTTER is a trademark and POTTER with colophon is a
registered trademark of Random House, Inc.

Originally published in Great Britain by Square Peg,
a division of The Random House Group Limited, London,
in 2010.

Library of Congress Cataloging-in-Publication Data
Crawford, Milton.
    The hungover cookbook / Milton Crawford.
    1. Hangover cures.   2. Hangover cures—Humor.
3. Cookbooks.   I. Title.
TX951.C763   2011
641.8'74—dc22   2010036939

ISBN 978-0-307-88631-6

Printed in China

10

First American Edition

I was left in no doubt about the
severity of the hangover when

a cat S T A M P E D

into the room.

P. G. Wodehouse

DON'T

PA

NIC!

hangover is an opportunity. I'll let that sink in for a moment. You may not be thinking this now, but by the time you put this book down I hope that you'll have changed your mind…

**A** hangover is an opportunity to see and taste the world in a new way. It's a chance for spontaneity and whimsical thoughts and deeds. Try something different. Try enjoying your hangover rather than simply enduring it. I'm going to show you how.

If it doesn't sound too grotesque to you in your weakened state, there is more than one way to skin a cat, and I will introduce to you the multi-faceted, subtle art of dealing with a hangover that goes far beyond the traditional British solution of chucking a full English at it.

And if you really can't be bothered—an attitude, by the way, that I entirely understand—just gobble some painkillers, drink some water, and head straight back to bed. But if you've got an appetite, then read on.

"Nothing in life is to be feared, it is only to be understood. Now is the time to understand more, so that we may fear less." Those were Marie Curie's words. I'm not sure whether she was thinking specifically about hangovers, but for the purposes of this book I'll assume that she was. You also do not need to be afraid, as I will help you to understand your beleaguered condition and to overcome it.

The hungover brain has regressed. It has been beaten into a state of infantile dependence. But it's that very state which suggests a chance at a break from the stale routines of adult life. This book aims to help you understand not only more about hangovers in general, but about your own individual hangover in particular. The process of discovery will be a glorious one: a hungover epiphany. That "the road of excess will lead to the palace of wisdom" might be a bit strong, but I hope that in some fun way your own individual egregiousness will help you to learn something and, most important, to feel a little better.

This book is a therapeutic cookbook, a gastronomic comedy, a burlesque homage to the possibility of snatching hope from failure, triumph from despair, laughter from tragedy.

Come; let us boldly step into this brave new world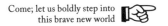

+

WHAT'S
THE
DIAGNOSIS

?

Hangovers are slightly more complex than you might at first think.

The famous comic writer P. G. Wodehouse came up with what is surely the definitive classification of hangover types in his Jeeves and Wooster novel *The Mating Season*. According to Wodehouse, there are six hangovers in all: the Broken Compass, the Sewing Machine, the Comet, the Atomic, the Cement Mixer and the Gremlin Boogie.

Each hangover type has its own specific characteristics. And before it's going to be possible to even think about tackling *your* hangover, you will need to work out what type of hangover you have. Bertie Wooster had his infinitely resourceful manservant Jeeves to help him get to grips with his morning-after wobbles, most often with his legendary pick-me-up drink that is discussed on page 40.

Unfortunately Jeeves is not at hand to help you. But Milton Crawford is at your service. And thankfully I have come up with a very short series of fun visual tests and a brief questionnaire that will help you to discover whether you are dizzy from the Cement Mixer or blown away by the Atomic.

Concept: Roger Shepard

How many legs does the elephant have?

a) .... Do you think that's important when I'm sinking into a mire of existential despair? Seven, perhaps?

b) .... I'm in too much pain to consider a question like this. But at first glance, two.

c) .... What a funny picture. Has it got five legs?

d) .... What?

e) .... Yuck! That's horrible. What's wrong with that elephant?

f) .... [unable to make a noise or even to fully open eyes]

Daer rdeaer,

It mghit aeppar at fsirt galcne taht tihs stenecne is raethr difclfiut to raed but it has been swhon, and pearhps you can aelrady see, taht as lnog as the fsirt and lsat leertts of a wrod are in tiher crreoct poonsitis tehn it soulhd be a ratelively strtforwaighard prositiopon for the rdeear to dphecier it, eevn if all the other ltteers are srablemcd. Taht's bsecaue redaers do not raed eervy lteetr wehn tehy raed a wrod; tehy sacn. Of curose this hpyoethsis no dbout rsets on the reaedr bneig in a cpaable state to raed an odinarry seenntce. And are you cpabale of eevn that at the mmeont, in your hoveungr sttae?

How long did it take you to understand this paragraph?

a) .... I still don't understand it now; I'm already tortured enough without you feeling the need to torture me further.

b) .... About five painful minutes.

c) .... Wow. How cool. Someone else had to explain it to me after half an hour but I see it perfectly now.

d) .... As long as it takes to read an ordinary sentence. Dumb-arse.

e) .... Reading regular text makes me want to vomit right now; that was like trying to read while standing on my head on a long bus journey. You disgust me.

f) .... grrrreeuughh [unidentified grunting noise]

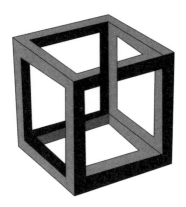

What is strange about this picture?

a) .... It's utterly confusing. It's an impossible shape.

b) .... The longer I look at it the more strange it appears, and looking at it from different angles reveals different possibilities as to what it might be.

c) .... It's a funny cube, isn't it? Like something by that Dutch mathematician.

d) .... Through the fog of my leviathan headache I can still work out that this picture supports two valid interpretations of how it can be seen (two different "types" of cube)—it's deliberately ambiguous and confusing, which is why it seems strange.

e) .... I'm going to be ill.

f) .... I. Am. Still. Alive. I think.

How many black dots do you see?

a) .... The whole page is full of black holes that I feel I may fall into at any moment.

b) .... I can't tell whether the dots are dots or whether they're prickly dot-sized pangs of pain in my head.

c) .... 25.

d) .... At first I see white dots. Then I look at a different part of the matrix and a sniper moves the black chasm of his gun barrel into position where the white dot was. Do they want to make my headache worse? Hang on; the rabbit has just jumped out of the hole: THERE ARE NO BLACK DOTS!

e) .... There is nothing more sick-making than shimmering black and white dots. Are there 12?

f) .... Nada. Nothing [taking pulse]. Oh, sorry, what was the question?

QUESTIONNAIRE

1. How does your head feel?

a) .... It's like I have four different brains all bickering with one another about who I am and what I should do next. It's giving me a headache.

b) .... Someone appears to be sneakily stabbing my head with something sharp—knitting needles, perhaps—while I'm not looking.

c) .... If it wasn't attached to my body by my neck, I feel that it would already have floated away by now.

d) .... A bomb has exploded inside my skull and all that's left is the drip, drip, drip of alcohol creating stalactites and stalagmites in my empty, aching cave of a cranium. My brain has disappeared completely.

e) .... I'm sorry; I missed that. I just stepped out of a washing machine on the spin cycle so will you please say that again? I'm really dizzy, by the way.

f) .... What, I still have a head?

2. How about your stomach?

a) .... I can't really tell. Sometimes it feels really great; totally top-notch and first rate, and other times it feels like something the dog's chewed on rather ruminatively before spitting it out on the carpet in disgust.

b) .... Strangely enough, the same person, or a collaborator thereof, who was sticking something sharp in my head has now turned their attention to my abdomen. Bastards!

c) .... Oh, fine, I think. I hadn't really thought about it; I was too busy dreaming about swimming with colorful fish in a tropical sea. I might be a bit gassy, though. Whoops!

d) .... So empty that I'm sure a really vacuous vacuum in the back of an empty warehouse in a deserted industrial estate in the most remote area of a forgotten city would have more in it than my stomach.

e) .... It's sloshing and churning; a ride in a rowing boat during an Atlantic storm in autumn would be calmer than my insides right now.

f) .... My stomach's currently staging a mutiny against the rest of my body. You'll have to ask me again later once I've (hopefully) reasserted control.

QUESTIONNAIRE

3. And, dear reader, how would you describe your mood?

a) .... Directionless. Broken. On the crumbling and precipitous outer edge of sanity. Life is completely and unmitigatingly meaningless.

b) .... Annoyed at how painful this whole thing is.

c) .... I'm just feeling rather… um… strange. Strange and light and woozy. And a bit giggly.

d) .... Damaged. Empty. And hungry.

e) .... Queasy and uneasy.

f) .... Destroyed. Utterly destroyed.

4. And what would your ideal activity be right now?

a) .... Painkillers and bed? At best I'll read a newspaper.

b) .... I just need to work out who I am and what I'm doing with my life. Until I've done that I can't see that there's any point in doing anything else.

c) .... I'd like to chat with my friends and look at some paintings, or watch films all day. Ice-skating could be fun.

d) .... I'm hungry. And I expect after I've eaten I'll fancy a drink.

e) .... Sitting quietly in a dark room until the swirling, swimming, spinning stops.

f) .... If I had a coffin, I'd go and lie in it.

5. What was the worst thing about last night?

a) .... I offended everyone with my inane bullshit and drunken monkey antics; when will I learn to control myself? I'm embarrassed.

b) .... The catastrophic impact on my bank balance.

c) .... There was nothing bad about it; I had a great time, and it's making me laugh still thinking about it now.

d) .... I don't remember a thing, which might be good or bad. I might find out which later.

e) .... Having a silly combination of drinks. Champagne, cider, whisky and Pernod is not a good mix.

f) .... Today.

THE DIAGNOSIS

I hope that the visual tests and questionnaire weren't too painful for you to complete. What it means is that I can now provide you with a definitive diagnosis based on your answers. You can use this diagnosis to find the recipes that will be right for your particular hungover state.

If you answered mainly **(a)**, you are almost certainly suffering from a Broken Compass, hence your lack of direction and certainty, and your general air of desperate confusion, restlessness, fear and loathing.

If you answered mainly **(b)**, the diagnosis is the Sewing Machine: Now you know why it feels like you're being stabbed in the head with sharp pointy things.

If you, dear space cadet, answered mainly **(c)**, you have the Comet, which is why you're swirling through space dust and are generally away with the fairies.

If you answered mainly **(d)**, you have the Atomic, hence the feeling of a nuclear explosion having detonated inside your skull.

If you answered mainly **(e)**, you have the deeply nauseating Cement Mixer.

And, poor little lamb, if you answered mainly **(f)**, you have the greatly feared and hugely distressing Gremlin Boogie.

THE
RECIPES

26 The Broken Compass

29.... Eggs Bhurji with fried bread

30.... Anna and Tommy's Mexican breakfast

32.... Pizza with yesterday's roast

34.... Shakshuka

36.... Deviled kidneys on toast

38.... Kedgeree

40.... Bloody Mary

42.... Huevos rancheros

44 The Sewing Machine

47.... The Elvis Presley peanut butter, banana and bacon sandwich

48.... Scrambled eggs with caramelized onion and feta cheese

50.... Leek, cheese and mustard mash with sausages and onion gravy

52.... The classic bacon sandwich

55.... Ice cream smoothie

56.... Croissants, Nutella and hot chocolate

58.... Boiled eggs with potato farl fingers

60 The Comet

63.... Stilton and pears on toast

64.... Lemon and demerara sugar pancakes

66.... Virgin piña colada

67.... Lemon lassi

68.... Lime soda

70.... Summer berries compote with Greek yogurt and granola

72.... The Knickerbocker Glory with Refreshers

74 The Atomic

77.... Chorizo omelette

78.... The breakfast burger

80.... Cardamom porridge with spicy apple sauce

82.... Potato hash with avocado and bacon

84.... Cheese, red onion and chutney toasties

86.... Spicy sausage and bean casserole

88.... Tagliatelle alla carbonara

90.... The English breakfast tortilla

92 The Cement Mixer

95.... A Turkish breakfast

96.... French toast with banana compote

98.... Milton Crawford's fish finger sandwich (with garlic green pea mayo)

100....Sweet lassi

102....The perfect tea and toast

104....Swiss rösti and poached eggs

106....Banana and passion fruit smoothie

108 The Gremlin Boogie

111.... Melon, feta, mint and ham salad

112.... Cheat's smoked salmon eggs Benedict

114.... Tahini and tomato toast

116.... Traditional Japanese breakfast

118.... Carrot, orange, apple and ginger juice

RATINGS I've designed all the recipes to be as easy and as quick as possible for hungover chefs who are in pain and have little patience. However, I've also rated each recipe so you can see which are particularly quick and easy, and which will take a little more time and effort.

....

THE HUNGOVER CHEF'S "DIFFICULTY" RATING

★ So easy that an agonizing headache and nausea will be no impediment

★★★★★ Loss of coordination, balance and will to live might make this recipe almost impossible; consider getting help

....

THE HUNGOVER CHEF'S "TIME" RATING

★ Quick enough to rescue you from doom in the blink of an eye

★★★★★ If you're feeling particularly weak, you may fade before you finish the recipe

Note All recipes are for two servings.

1

THE COMPASS BROKEN

The Broken Compass is a distinctly psychological type of hangover, one that Kingsley Amis might have described as being profoundly metaphysical. He wrote, in his authoritative and masterly tome on the subject of alcohol, *On Drink,* that the Metaphysical Hangover combines "that ineffable compound of depression, sadness (these two are not the same), anxiety, self-hatred, sense of failure and fear for the future." You also feel utterly directionless and indecisive. Everything you do is destined to be futile today, or at least that's how you feel at the moment. Going back to bed may feel like the best remedy, but I recommend action over inaction, positive thinking over maudlin self-pity and a menu of spicy comfort food to reignite your passion for life, such as Mexican, or ranch-style eggs *(huevos rancheros)* and a highly charged, pepped-up variety of Bloody (or virgin) Mary. Try some self-maintenance, like a hot shower, a shave, some cutting of fingernails and a quick vacuum around the house (if your head doesn't hurt too much). It'll make you feel constructive and give you a sense of direction and self-worth, something that will be further enhanced by spicy scram that pulls no punches. Life does have meaning; you just need some spice to make things nice.

EGGS BHURJHI WITH FRIED BREAD

2 tbsp unsalted butter

—

1 tsp mustard seeds

—

a few small curry leaves

—

2 spring onions, finely chopped

—

½ tsp grated ginger

—

½ hot green chili pepper, de-seeded and very thinly sliced

—

pinch of turmeric

—

½ tsp ground cumin powder

—

1 tomato, skinned and diced

—

4 free-range eggs, beaten

—

fried bread or buttered toast, for serving

DIFFICULTY: ★ TIME: ★★

When I was in southern India a wonderful woman called Ratti made this dish for me at her home in the wild forests of Karnataka. Ratti is the best and most hard-working cook I have ever met. Thinking about her food brings tears to my eyes (and not just at the thought of all the chili she used). This recipe is essentially spicy scrambled eggs and is very easy to make, though I'm sure it will never be quite as good as the way she cooked it.

Ratti served it with rice roti (rice-flour bread), but she also made great fried bread and this is what I recommend you have with your eggs, though buttered toast also works well.

Milton's method ☞ Melt the butter in a frying pan over medium heat. Add the mustard seeds, stir once, then add the curry leaves and spring onion and cook for a couple of minutes until the onion is soft.

Stir in the ginger, chili, turmeric, cumin powder and diced tomato and gently fry for a couple of minutes, stirring occasionally, before adding the beaten eggs.

Turn the heat down to low and cook, stirring occasionally, until the eggs are set. Serve immediately on fried bread or buttered toast.

ANNA AND TOMMY'S MEXICAN BREAKFAST

olive oil,
for frying

—

½ onion, finely
chopped

—

1 garlic clove,
crushed

—

½ green chili
pepper, de-seeded
and chopped

—

4 Polish kabanos
sausages, chopped
into small pieces

—

3 medium-sized
tomatoes, chopped

—

2 soft-flour or
corn tortillas

—

2 free-range eggs

—

handful of
grated aged
cheddar cheese

—

a few jalapeño
peppers (best
from a jar),
to taste

—

salt and black
pepper

DIFFICULTY: ★ TIME: ★★

This recipe comes courtesy of two of my favorite boozing companions, whom I've accompanied to many pubs and other drinking salons in London, from Gipsy Hill to Stoke Newington, and further afield. We've never made it to Mexico for a binge, but there seems little reason to bother when they have brought Mexico to me, albeit in a slightly unorthodox fashion—via Poland—in the form of this fantastically hearty and spicy recipe.

Milton's method ☞ Heat a little oil in a frying pan over medium to high heat. Add the onion and cook until it has slightly colored and softened, then stir in the garlic and chili and cook for a further minute.

Add the chopped sausage to the pan and fry for about five minutes, stirring occasionally. Stir in the chopped tomatoes, bring to the boil, then turn down the heat and simmer for another five minutes or so.

Heat the tortillas in the oven or under the broiler, according to the packet instructions.

While the tortillas are heating, fry the eggs in a little oil in a separate frying pan.

Place the hot tortillas on plates, taking care not to burn your fingers. Ladle the sausage and tomato mixture on the middle of each tortilla, but not too near the edges; you don't want any filling to leak out later. Top with the grated cheese and a few jalapeño peppers to taste. Carefully fold in the sides of each tortilla, then fold down the top and fold up the bottom, to form a parcel.

Place a fried egg on top of each parcel. Season with salt and black pepper and serve immediately.

If your wife or other partner is beside you, and (of course) is willing, perform the sexual act as

V_I GO^ROUSLY as you can.

The exercise will do you good, and—on the assumption that you enjoy sex—you will feel toned up emotionally...

Warnings: (1) if you are in bed with somebody you should not be in bed with, and have *in the least degree* a bad conscience about this, abstain. Guilt and shame are prominent constituents of the Metaphysical Hangover, and will certainly be sharpened by indulgence on such an occasion... (2) For the same generic reason, do not take the matter into your own hands if you awake by yourself.

Kingsley Amis
(From *On Drink*, Jonathan Cape, London, 1972)

PIZZA WITH YESTERDAY'S ROAST

2 ready-made
pizza crusts,
defrosted if
frozen
—
3½ oz freshly
grated parmesan
or grana padano
cheese, to serve

For the tomato
sauce:
—
olive oil, for
frying
—
3 fat cloves
garlic, crushed
and finely
chopped
—
1 tbsp balsamic
vinegar
—
1 14-oz can
good-quality
tomatoes
—
1 tbsp tomato
purée
—
1 tsp dried
oregano

DIFFICULTY: ★ TIME: ★★

Making your own pizza crusts is a somewhat messy,
though certainly rewarding activity, but for this
wonderfully simple "recipe" (easy for even the laziest
of hungover chefs) I buy cheap-as-chips, ready-
made pizza crusts from the supermarket to adorn
with the remains of yesterday's roast. It's best to use
meat that has not got too dry; well-done beef or dry
pork will be even drier (perhaps unpalatably so) once
it has been fired on top of your Italian chapatti.
Feel free to add some chopped bacon (small pieces
of streaky lardons or pancetta are best) or sausage,
chopped small, into the mix as well.

I find that a homemade, garlicky tomato sauce
topped with spicy leftover meat and pickled chilis
is an irresistibly tantalizing combination for the
hungover palate. I hope you agree.

Milton's method ☞ If using frozen pizza crusts, make
sure they have thawed out.

To make the tomato sauce, heat some oil in a
frying pan over low to medium heat. Add the garlic
and cook gently for about one minute, stirring all the
while, so that the garlic doesn't color, but flavors the
oil. Add the balsamic vinegar carefully, as the pan
will spit, and let it reduce for about 3–4 minutes. Stir
in the tomatoes and the tomato purée, bring to a
boil and add the oregano, then reduce the heat and
simmer on a very low heat for about 20 minutes,
stirring occasionally, until the mixture is thick,
almost sticky.

For the spicy
meat topping:

olive oil, for
frying

—

4 pickled
jalapeño peppers
(from a jar), cut
in half

—

approx. ½ lb
leftover roast
meat (beef, lamb,
chicken or pork;
see above), cut
into bite-sized
pieces

—

½ sweet red bell
pepper, de-seeded
and chopped

—

½ green chili,
de-seeded and
finely chopped

—

handful of pitted
black olives, cut
in half

—

salt and pepper
to taste

Preheat the oven to 425°F.

To make the spicy meat topping, heat some oil in a separate frying pan over a high heat. Throw the halved jalapeño peppers into the hot oil, then add the roast meat, sweet pepper, chopped chili, olives, and salt and pepper to taste, and flash-fry for a couple of minutes, making sure all the meat gets a light coating of oil.

To assemble the pizzas, spread the tomato sauce evenly over your pizza crusts, then divide the meat mixture between them, making sure that the halved chilis are distributed equally across both bases.

Put on the top shelf of the oven and bake for about 15 minutes, or until the pizza crusts are crisp.

Remove the pizzas from the oven, sprinkle the cheese over them and serve with a crisp green salad and, if you're up to it, an ice-cold beer.

SHAKSHUKA

good slug of
olive oil (about
2 tbsp)

—

½ onion, diced

—

2 bay leaves

—

1 jalapeño
pepper, de-seeded
and finely sliced

—

½ red sweet
bell pepper,
de-seeded and
chopped

—

2 garlic cloves,
crushed and
chopped

—

1 tsp ground
cumin

—

1 tsp smoked hot
(spicy) paprika

—

1 14-oz can
chopped tomatoes

—

pinch of superfine
sugar

DIFFICULTY: ★★ TIME: ★★★

The name doesn't readily roll off the tongue on
a hungover morning but this recipe, which uses
a combination of eggs and spicy tomato sauce—
similar to the Mexican *huevos rancheros* (see page
42), though with a distinctively North African/
Middle Eastern flavor—offers a memorably fiery
blast-off to a day that might otherwise have proved
drab and dull.

Shakshuka is usually thought of as an Israeli
breakfast dish, but in fact is eaten widely in
Morocco, Tunisia, Algeria and Yemen, too. The
only slightly unusual ingredient is the smoked
paprika, which gives the tomato sauce a wonderful
smoky richness.

This version is quite spicy; if you prefer a milder
dish, you can halve the quantities of jalapeño
pepper and paprika.

Milton's method ☞ Heat the olive oil in a frying
pan over medium heat and cook the onion for
5–7 minutes, stirring occasionally, until the onion
has softened and taken on a slight golden color.

Add the bay leaves, jalapeño pepper, red pepper
and garlic, and stir. Keep stirring and cook for a
further minute.

Add the cumin and paprika and continue stirring
for a further minute.

*salt and pepper
to taste*

—

*4 free-range
eggs*

—

*2 large pita
breads, cut in
half*

—

*a few leaves
flat-leaf parsley,
to garnish*

Stir in the tomatoes and a pinch of superfine sugar, season with salt and pepper to taste, and leave to simmer on a low heat for about seven minutes, stirring occasionally.

When the sauce has thickened, make four small "craters" in the tomato mixture and break one egg into each crater in turn.

Leave the mixture on low heat for 2 minutes, until the egg whites begin to set, then place the frying pan under a medium broiler for 3–4 minutes, keeping a careful watch to make sure the egg yolks don't fully set: runny yolks are essential.

Take the frying pan out from under the broiler, season the eggs to taste with salt and pepper, and set aside while you toast the pita breads.

Toast the pita breads under the broiler.

Lift the eggs out of the sauce, placing two on each plate and spoon the sauce alongside, removing the bay leaves. Garnish with a little flat-leaf parsley. Place the pita breads on the side of each plate and make sure you use them to dip into the delicious sauce.

DEVILED KIDNEYS
ON TOAST

5 lamb's kidneys

—

pat of butter

—

salt and pepper to taste

—

4 thick slices white bread

—

a little olive oil, for brushing the bread

—

small handful of flat-leaf parsley, washed and roughly chopped

For the sauce:

1 tbsp tomato purée

—

1½ tsp English mustard

—

1 tsp lemon juice

—

½ tsp cayenne pepper

DIFFICULTY: ★★★ TIME: ★★

This classic breakfast dish, redolent of Edwardian Britain, delivers a big, satisfyingly spicy, meaty hit, although dicing slippery lamb's kidneys on a hungover morning might not agree with everyone's constitution. This version is fairly spicy; if you prefer a milder flavor, reduce the cayenne pepper to a pinch and the English mustard to half a teaspoon.

It's important to use thick slices of bread for the toast. I recommend you brush the bread with olive oil and cook on a ridged griddle pan, but you could just as easily toast your bread and then butter it before serving the kidney mixture onto it.

Milton's method ☞ Remove the skin from the lamb's kidneys and, using a sharp knife, chop the kidneys in half lengthways. Now, use a pair of scissors to cut out the small white core, then cut the kidneys into small dice. Careful: they're slippery!

Make up the sauce in a medium-sized bowl by whisking the ingredients together thoroughly with a fork or egg whisk.

Melt the butter in a frying pan over medium to high heat. At the same time, if you have a ridged griddle pan, start warming the pan over a high heat.

Once the butter in the frying pan has melted, throw in the kidneys and sauté them for about 3–4 minutes, until they are a golden brown color.

Add the whisked sauce to the frying pan and stir thoroughly to ensure that all the kidneys get coated with the sauce. Season with salt and pepper, then turn the heat down slightly and simmer for a further 3–4 minutes.

If using a griddle pan, brush the slices of bread with oil then press them down onto the hot pan (or simply toast the bread under the broiler and then butter it before serving). Once the bread has golden lines burnt into it on both sides, transfer to serving plates and immediately spoon the kidneys and sauce onto it. Sprinkle the flat-leaf parsley over the kidneys, to garnish.

KEDGEREE

DIFFICULTY: ★★★ TIME: ★★★★

2 free-range eggs

—

1½ tbsp unsalted butter

—

olive oil, for frying

—

1 medium onion, very finely sliced

—

1 garlic clove, crushed

—

1½ tbsp fresh ginger, peeled and grated

—

5 black peppercorns, left whole

—

½ tsp ground turmeric

—

½ tsp ground cumin

—

4 green cardamom pods, lightly crushed and left whole

—

3½ oz white basmati rice

Kedgeree is a versatile comfort-food dish—perfect for a hungover breakfast, but good at any time of day. The prawns are optional and not to everyone's taste in the morning.

Milton's method ☞ Start by boiling the eggs—hard-boiled is best for this recipe; allow 6–8 minutes. Run cold water over the eggs, and leave to cool before peeling and quartering.

Heat the butter with some oil in a deep frying pan over medium heat, and cook the onion until soft. Add the garlic, ginger, peppercorns and the dry spices. Stir well, then reduce the heat and continue to cook on very low heat for about 15 minutes, stirring occasionally to prevent burning; remove the pan from the heat if the contents become too dry.

Meanwhile, rinse the rice thoroughly in several changes of cold water. Heat a scant tablespoon of oil in a heavy-based saucepan and add the rice, stirring until it becomes translucent. Add boiling water to a fingernail's depth above the rice, then tightly fit a double layer of foil over the pan, and cover with a lid. Cook on very low heat for 20 minutes, or until all the water is absorbed and the rice is fluffy.

½ lb undyed
smoked haddock

—

12 large peeled
raw tiger
prawns, fresh
or frozen
(optional)

—

½ cup or more
fish stock (use
cooking liquid
from haddock)

To finish:

1–2 tbsp mild
korma curry
paste

—

½ cup crème
fraîche

—

chopped fresh
parsley (optional)

While the rice is cooking, put the smoked
haddock in a separate pan, cover with boiling water
and simmer gently for 10 minutes. Using a fish slice,
remove the haddock to a dish, leaving the cooking
water in the pan. Let the haddock cool slightly
before removing the skin, then flake the fish with
a fork and remove any bones.

Add the prawns (if using) to the fish cooking-
water, and simmer until they turn pink. Remove
the prawns and add to the flaked fish, reserving the
cooking liquid.

Gently stir the cooked rice into the onion and
spice mixture, adding ½ cup or more of the reserved
fish stock. Add the flaked fish and prawns (if
using) to the rice and, finally, stir in the korma
paste and crème fraîche.

Serve immediately, topping each portion with a
quartered egg, and sprinkle with the chopped
parsley (if using).

BLOODY MARY

2¼ cups good-quality tomato juice

—

½ cup vodka

—

1 tbsp ketchup

—

1 tsp lemon juice

—

½ tbsp Worcestershire sauce

—

splash of Tabasco, or to taste

—

small pinch of hot (spicy) smoked paprika

—

celery salt (or sea salt if you don't have celery salt)

—

freshly ground black pepper

DIFFICULTY: ★ TIME: ★

There are as many Bloody Mary recipes as there are drinkers of Bloody Marys: everyone has their own twist or variation on the classic hangover pick-me-up. I'm not claiming to have the definitive version with this recipe, as much is up to personal preference, but I like it.

Wodehouse's legendary manservant, Jeeves, had a pick-me-up that some have speculated was like a Bloody Mary, but with a raw egg yolk added. So, throw in an egg if you like, but my recipe eschews it in favor of more traditional ingredients, all fairly conventional—apart, perhaps, from the ketchup, which Kingsley Amis described as "the secret of the whole thing" although he was "not all clear on what it does, but it does something considerable."

Of course, a Bloody Mary is no more a cure for a hangover than is a pint of lager: all it does is top up the levels of alcohol in the bloodstream, and sooner or later you might want to return to having no alcohol whatsoever in your bloodstream; even I try this from time to time. So feel free to make a "virgin" Mary by dispensing with the vodka altogether.

To serve:

ice

—

*2 sticks celery
(if you really
have to)*

The celery stick is often seen as obligatory but I've yet to meet anyone who actually enjoys gnawing on celery when they have a hangover; add it only if you need something to scratch your back with.

Milton's method ☞ Combine all the ingredients in a large pitcher and mix thoroughly to make sure that the ketchup is fully absorbed into the tomato juice.

Adjust the seasoning, adding more celery salt or black pepper to taste. Serve over ice, in tall glasses, give a quick stir and plop a celery stick in each glass, if desired.

HUEVOS RANCHEROS

olive oil

—

1 onion, diced

—

1 large garlic
clove, very
thinly sliced

—

1 green chili
pepper, de-seeded
and chopped

—

1 14-oz can
chopped tomatoes

—

handful of
coriander,
chopped

—

salt and pepper

—

1 can refried
beans

—

4 corn tortillas

—

4 free-range
eggs

—

1 lime

—

1 red chili pepper,
de-seeded and
finely sliced
(to garnish)

DIFFICULTY: ★★★ TIME: ★★

This classic Mexican dish of ranch-style eggs,
served with crispy tortillas, refried beans and
a spicy tomato salsa, guarantees a spicy start to
the day.

I generally prefer to cook things from scratch,
but to do this with the refried beans requires
good organizational skills, and I've assumed
that yours may be in some disarray. So, I
recommend you get a can of refried beans to
reheat. They add something great to this dish,
in particular a very pleasing texture.

Milton's method ☞ Heat a little oil in a frying pan
or wok and gently fry the onion, garlic and green
chili for about five minutes, until the onion is
softened but not colored.

Add the tomatoes and half the coriander to
the pan, and season with salt and pepper to taste.
Simmer for about 15 minutes, until the mixture
has thickened slightly.

Meanwhile, preheat the oven to 425°F, and
gently heat the refried beans in a saucepan over
medium heat.

Lightly brush the tortillas with oil. Place
directly on a rack in the oven for approximately
10 minutes, until golden and slightly crispy.

In a separate, heavy-bottomed pan, fry the eggs
gently in a little olive oil.

Just before serving, add a squeeze of lime juice
to the tomato salsa, and stir in.

To serve, place two tortillas on each plate (slightly warmed). Spread a quarter of the refried beans on each tortilla, followed by a little salsa, and top with the fried eggs. Spoon the rest of the salsa on and around the eggs. Garnish with the remaining coriander and the sliced red chili, and serve with wedges of lime.

There is nothing quite like a masala dosa as a meal for almost any type of hangover, but for the Broken Compass it's especially good. The masala dosa—a form of crispy rice-flour pancake with a spicy potato filling—comes from southern India and is especially popular in Tamil Nadu. It's usually served, often at breakfast, with coconut chutney and a spicy vegetable curry called sambar. It's probably not the ideal dish to cook with a hangover, particularly if you are cooking it for the first time, as it requires a couple of specialist ingredients and, to be properly authentic, some unusual cooking equipment. It's also a bit tricky.

I therefore recommend that you go hunting for your dosa either with your telephone (by calling a local takeout) or in person by visiting, if you're lucky enough to have one within staggering distance, your local south Indian restaurant. If you're struggling to talk, some restaurants now accept online orders. Other types of Indian restaurants and takeout joints may also be able to rustle up a dosa for you even if it's not on the menu. Ask.

The wonderful combination of textures—the crispy pancake on the outside, with the soft, billowy, spicy mashed potato inside—makes it ideal comfort food and a very wholesome way to start the day.

2

THE SEWING MACHINE

Oh cruel, cruel world in which the slings and arrows of outrageous fortune seem today to all be directed at you. But there is something more insistent and precise about these slings and arrows, a repetitive, mechanical urgency to the suffering that is being inflicted on you. There is a needle. You know there's a needle because you can feel it. It's a long needle and it's very sharp. It's jabbing you with military precision at various points in your head, sometimes right between your eyes, sometimes in your temples, and sometimes in the top of your skull, which today feels as thin and as delicate as an eggshell. This is what P. G. Wodehouse called the Sewing Machine, a particularly sadistic form of hangover that will prove irritatingly distracting. And it hurts. Painkillers and rehydration are the obvious answers. But you also need something to eat that is soothing and comforting, something to ease away the sharp, forbidding pain of the sewing machine: food that feels like wrapping yourself in a thick duvet away from the relentlessly stabbing onslaught. Try these ultimate comfort-food recipes; they'll make you feel like you've nestled into the coziest bed imaginable. And remember that a lack of sleep makes you more sensitive to pain, so perhaps after you've eaten you might want to get a little more shut-eye. Ahhh, there you go; better already.

THE ELVIS PRESLEY PEANUT BUTTER, BANANA AND BACON SANDWICH

4 thick slices
good-quality
fresh white
bread

—

2 tbsp crunchy
peanut butter

—

1 banana,
mashed with
the back of a fork

—

1 tbsp honey

—

8 slices free-range
streaky bacon

—

butter, for frying
(optional)

DIFFICULTY: ★ TIME: ★★

This sandwich is, of course, in very dubious taste. But exercising dubious taste is all part of the whimsical hungover experience. And, anyway, this post-modern hymn to American excess between two slices of bread, this portion of rock and roll history, this hearty helping of artery-clogging flimflam, is far more than a mere sandwich—it is a legend.

Milton's method ☞ Thickly spread each slice of bread with the peanut butter. Cover two slices with the mashed banana and drizzle with honey.

Grill the bacon until crispy then place on top of the banana, dividing it between the two slices of bread. Top each sandwich with a second slice of bread. For extra calorific value (and authenticity), carefully fry each sandwich in butter.

If this sandwich becomes a habit, get friendly with a cardiac surgeon. You may need one.

SCRAMBLED EGGS WITH CARAMELIZED ONION AND FETA CHEESE

2 tbsp unsalted butter

—

dash of olive oil

—

1 medium-sized onion, finely chopped

—

½ tsp superfine sugar

—

4 free-range eggs, beaten

—

3 tbsp whole milk

—

4½ oz feta cheese

—

small handful of finely chopped chives, plus 4 whole chives to garnish

—

freshly ground black pepper

—

4 slices toast with butter, to serve

DIFFICULTY: ★★ TIME: ★★

Here, the sweetness of the caramelized onion matched with the salty yet creamy feta cheese is a wonderful combination. It's also, of course, cheese and onion, one of the greatest pairings since Adam and Eve, not to mention Bogart and Bacall, or Boswell and Johnson. A classic, in other words.

And it's a good recipe for those people who don't like their eggs too eggy, something that will make sense to some hungover readers but not to others.

Milton's method ☞ Put a frying pan over medium high heat and add the butter and oil. When the butter has melted, add the onion and superfine sugar, and cook for 15–20 minutes, making sure that all the onion gets coated by the butter-oil mixture so it gets nice and caramelized. Be careful not to let the onion burn: you will need to stir occasionally but not too much. Once the onion begins to brown, turn the heat down slightly to medium.

Meanwhile, beat the eggs with the milk. Then, when the onions have a rich golden color, reduce the heat to low and add the beaten eggs to the pan. Cook slowly, stirring occasionally, for about five minutes.

Once the eggs begin to take on a slightly firmer consistency, add half the feta cheese and gently stir it into the egg and onion mixture. Cook for another two minutes or so, until the eggs are reasonably firm but not too dry, then throw in the chopped chives.

Serve immediately on the buttered toast, crumbling the remaining feta over the top and garnishing each portion with some pepper and a couple of whole chives.

LEEK, CHEESE AND MUSTARD MASH WITH SAUSAGES AND ONION GRAVY

1½ lbs floury potatoes (such as Idaho)

—

5 tbsp unsalted butter

—

1 small leek, washed and split in half lengthways then chopped

—

6 good-quality free-range pork sausages

—

1 onion, finely sliced

—

1 tbsp all-purpose flour

—

1¼ cups vegetable or chicken stock

—

2 tbsp milk

—

1 tbsp wholegrain mustard, plus extra for serving

—

2 oz aged cheddar cheese, grated

—

2 oz canned unsweetened unsalted corn

—

salt and pepper

DIFFICULTY: ★★★ TIME: ★★★

The point of this dish is that the mash—that supreme comfort food—is king; not the sausages, which are merely courtiers to bow and scrape before the mighty tuber. This is no ordinary mash. Mash purists may shudder and reflexively grab their spuds (or, at the very least, call it "champ"), but for me the combination of buttered leeks, tangy mustard, extra-mature cheddar and corn, wrapped in the billowy folds of Sir Walter Raleigh's finest, is an unparalleled delight.

The sausages (I use free-range ones from outdoor-bred pigs) are, nonetheless, an enjoyable sideshow and to stop the whole thing getting too dry, I envelop them in shimmering, velvety, pale onion gravy (not the dark brown stuff you get in gastro-pubs) and serve it with hot English mustard. A real treat.

Milton's method ☞ Peel the potatoes and cut each one evenly in half, so that all the pieces are of a similar size. Place the potatoes in a heavy-bottomed saucepan and cover them with cold water. Using your hands, mix the potatoes in the saucepan until the water becomes cloudy, then drain the potatoes, either using the saucepan lid or through a colander, and return to the pan. Repeat this process.

Now, pour cold water over the potatoes in the pan, just enough to cover them; add a little salt, put a lid on the pan and place over high heat.

While the potatoes are coming to the boil, heat a frying pan over a low heat and melt 1½ tbsp of the butter in it. Add the leek and gently sauté for about 10 minutes, stirring occasionally, until the leek is soft, then remove from the heat and set aside.

Put the sausages under a preheated broiler, and cook for 10–15 minutes, turning them occasionally so they cook on all sides.

Meanwhile, in a separate, small frying pan, heat another 1½ tbsp of butter and cook the onion for about 15 minutes, until it has slightly colored and softened. Add the flour, and stir until it is absorbed into the mixture, then add the vegetable or chicken stock, a little at a time, stirring continuously until all the stock is added. Keep the heat on low and let the gravy thicken somewhat. Season to taste with salt and pepper.

Once the potatoes have come to a boil, cook for about 15 minutes or until they are fully cooked but not crumbling. Take them off the heat, drain, then return to the pan and put over low heat for a couple of minutes to dry them out slightly. With the pan still on the heat, add the remaining 2 tbsp of butter along with the milk and some salt and pepper, and mash until all lumps have been removed. Add the leeks, mustard, cheese and corn and stir through thoroughly, using a fork.

Serve the mash alongside the sausages. Pour the gravy over the sausages and add a dollop of mustard.

THE CLASSIC BACON SANDWICH

6 slices free-range
dry-cured bacon
—
4 thick slices
fresh white
bread
—
ketchup (home-
made is best),
to serve

DIFFICULTY: ★ TIME: ★

I know what you're thinking: How difficult is it to make a bacon sandwich? Well, yes, there's little doubt that one of its main attributes for the hungover chef is its simplicity of execution: you cook the bacon, insert between two slices of bread, add sauce to taste, *et voilà*.

But the fact that it's so simple means, for me, that if you make a mistake, it's all the more obvious. There are only two basic things that you need for a great bacon sandwich: good-quality bacon, perfectly cooked; and very fresh, soft, fluffy white bread. Everything else is optional. I'm not going to get too prescriptive here, as much of the bacon sandwich experience is down to personal preference—grilled or fried, smoked or unsmoked, ketchup or brown sauce, and so on. But you should not adulterate a bacon sandwich with lettuce, tomato or mayonnaise. It is no longer a bacon sandwich; it is a BLT, which is an entirely different thing.

Milton's method ☞ Broil the bacon. That sounds like the healthy option, but I suggest you tuck one of the pieces of bread underneath the bacon so that the fat drips down onto it and it gets slightly toasted, which makes it rather less healthy.

Cook the bacon until the fat turns crispy but not so much that the meat dries out; the bacon should still have a pinkish color, not brown.

Serve immediately between the bread, with no butter, and a little ketchup.

I may be drunk,
Madam, but in
the morning I
will be sober and

you will still be

UGLY

Winston Churchill

ICE CREAM SMOOTHIE

1 batch summer berries compote, made with 18 oz berries (page 70)

—

6 scoops good-quality vanilla ice cream, plus 2 scoops to garnish

—

2 sprigs fresh mint

DIFFICULTY: ★★ TIME: ★

To make this indulgent smoothie, I use the summer berries compote recipe on page 70 along with some good-quality vanilla ice cream.

Milton's method ☞ Put the fruit compote and six scoops of ice cream into a blender and process very briefly by pulsing the blender on and off two or three times.

Serve immediately in tall glasses, with long spoons for eating, adding an extra scoop of ice cream on top of each smoothie and a sprig of fresh mint.

CROISSANTS, NUTELLA AND HOT CHOCOLATE

4 good-quality croissants

—

1 jar Nutella hazelnut chocolate spread

For the hot chocolate:

5 cups whole milk

—

8 oz good-quality dark chocolate (min. 70% cocoa), broken into small pieces

—

1 tbsp superfine sugar (optional)

—

whipped cream from a can

—

cocoa powder, for dusting

DIFFICULTY: ★ TIME: ★

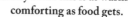

I scrupulously avoid caffeine with a hangover, as I find it merely makes me nervous and even more dehydrated than I already am. A great alternative to tea and coffee is hot chocolate, which in Britain still suffers a slight image problem as a brew for spinsters and librarians (and probably spinster librarians). It is far more widely drunk across the rest of Europe, though, where they evidently appreciate the undeniable joy of imbibing liquid chocolate.

Chocolate is a feel-good food which triggers the release of endorphins in the brain, and there's no better way to improve your mood than to drink and eat it at the same time with this very typical French breakfast. There's not much to do here except to make good hot chocolate, warm up your croissants in the oven, slather on the Nutella spread and dip your chocolatey crescent into your chocolatey milk: this is as warmly comforting as food gets.

Milton's method ☞ Preheat the oven to 375°F, for warming the croissants later.

Warm 1¼ cups of milk in a saucepan over a low heat and add the broken-up chocolate. Stir continuously until the chocolate has melted, then add the rest of the milk. Keep the pan on the heat, stirring regularly, for about five minutes, but don't let it boil. Add the sugar if you like your hot chocolate slightly sweeter.

Meanwhile, heat the croissants in the hot oven for about five minutes, then slather on the Nutella.

Serve the hot chocolate in bowls that can be lifted to your lips with both hands. Finish with a squirt of whipped cream on top and a dusting of cocoa powder.

Dip and sup your way through your croissants and hot chocolate and by the end I guarantee that you will not only feel warm inside, you'll be glowing with pleasure.

BOILED EGGS WITH
POTATO FARL FINGERS

mashed potato (made from about 1 lb white potatoes), with a fairly solid consistency

—

2 tbsp unsalted butter, plus extra for greasing

—

salt and pepper

—

4 tbsp all-purpose flour, plus extra for kneading

—

4 free-range eggs

DIFFICULTY: ★★★ TIME: ★★★★

This is a great way of using up leftover mashed potato. Dipping these lovely fingers, or "soldiers," of buttery potato pancake into soft-boiled eggs is extremely soothing: comfort food at its very best.

Milton's method ☞ Either make the mashed potato from scratch or, even better, use leftover mashed potato from the fridge. A fairly solid consistency is desirable. Preheat the oven to 475°F.

Place the mashed potato in a saucepan over low heat. Add the butter and some salt and pepper if required, then fold in the flour until it is fully combined with the potato. The mixture will stick together and start to resemble a ball of dough.

Remove the "dough" from the saucepan and knead it with a little extra flour. Roll out the dough to a thickness of approximately ⅛ inch, and cut it into fingers, each about 3 x 1 inch. You should be able to get about 20 fingers or so: 10 per serving.

Place a buttered baking tray on top of the stove over medium heat and place the fingers in it. Once the farls start to sizzle, pop the tray into the oven for about 15 minutes, turning once halfway through.

In the meantime, boil your eggs—soft-boiled is essential (somewhere between three and five minutes on a rolling boil).

The potato farls are ready when they are a golden brown color and crisp on the outside. Serve them immediately, still hot, with a bit of butter if you like, alongside the eggs with their tops lopped off.

The chippy, with its stench of cooking fat, hot batter and raw fish, might not sound like the best place to visit with a hangover, but good fishcakes with chips and mushy peas is arguably one of the better comfort foods you can have, though clearly not the healthiest. Essential equipment, therefore, could include a clothespin for your nose if you feel that your sensitivity to smell might bring on a bout of nausea.

Very few fish and chip shops do home deliveries, but it's worth checking whether yours does. The only thing you need to make your meal complete is the addition of some tartar sauce and ketchup as well as thick hunks of bread—brown or white, according to your preference—smothered with butter. For an old-fashioned twist, drink a pot of tea while you're chowing down.

3

You are enveloped in a fuzzy atmosphere of stardust, ice, rock and gases. In many ways you feel fine. But you also feel indistinct and occasionally, though not horribly so, a little hysterical. You sense that you've somehow lost a direct connection with the world. "Planet earth is blue, and there's nothing I can do" is the kind of line from a song that might whirr around your brain incessantly. Then again, it could be any line from any song or even just a single thought that seems to be stuck in your brain, like "who the hell invented Tuesdays?" Douglas Adams, in his *Hitchhiker's Guide to the Galaxy*, wrote about a particularly potent cocktail called the Pan-Galactic Gargle Blaster, that drinking it was "like having your brains smashed out by a slice of lemon wrapped round a large gold brick." Now, that still sounds fairly painful to me. There's no doubt that your hangover may share the more surreal aspects of this description, but less of the severe pain. To be frank, you need something to cut through this type of cosmic crap— try these recipes with fizz, sparkle and bite.

STILTON AND PEARS ON TOAST

4 slices brown
or whole-grain
bread
—
a little
unsalted butter
—
1 ripe pear,
peeled, cored
and cut into thin
slices
—
8 oz good Stilton
—
freshly ground
black pepper

To serve:

plum chutney
—
handful of
endive leaves

DIFFICULTY ★ TIME: ★

This is a nice take on cheese on toast: the sharp, creamy Stilton is guaranteed to invigorate your tired taste buds and the warm, sweet pear forms a delicious counterpoint.

Milton's method ☞ Lightly toast the bread and butter it.

Layer the pear slices on each slice of toast so they cover as much of it as possible. Crumble the Stilton over the top.

Place under the broiler for about five minutes, until the Stilton has melted and is beginning to brown and bubble. Season with a little pepper.

Serve immediately with some plum chutney and a few endive leaves.

LEMON AND DEMERARA SUGAR PANCAKES

Makes approx. 8 thin pancakes

For the batter:

4 oz all-purpose flour

—

pinch of salt

—

1 cup whole milk

—

⅓ cup water

—

2 medium free-range eggs

—

1 tbsp unsalted butter, melted and cooled

—

butter, for frying

To serve:

2 oz demerara sugar

—

juice of 2 lemons

—

1 tbsp grated lemon zest (from an unwaxed lemon)

DIFFICULTY: ★★★ TIME: ★★★

I once went, with a particularly severe hangover, to one of those megastores in some kind of semi-industrialized, out-of-town wasteland. You know the type of store I mean—the sort that sells DIY stuff or Swedish-designed, Chinese-manufactured, self-assembly furniture, or car parts and bicycles. Whatever else you do with your hangover, don't go to any of these places; they are enervating and soul-destroying.

To get over the shock of this expedition I downed a small glass of schnapps on my return (which I had pre-poured and left inside the freezer for just such an emergency) and set about making thin pancakes—crêpes, really—with sugar and lemon to warm my frozen soul.

Milton's method ☞ Sift the flour and salt into a bowl. In a separate bowl, combine the milk and water. Make a well in the flour and add the two eggs. Beat them into the flour, using a wooden spoon, then gradually add the milk and water mixture, stirring continuously until you have a smooth batter. Stir in the melted butter.

Put a 6-inch non-stick frying pan over a high heat. When the pan is hot, add a pat of butter. Once the butter has melted, add enough batter to thinly coat the surface of the frying pan and cook for about one minute, until the bottom of the pancake is firm and golden, before flipping it over, either with a deft flick of the wrist or using a slice. Cook for a further minute or so, then remove to a warmed plate and cover with foil to keep warm. Repeat the process with the remaining batter.

You can eat your pancakes with a knife and fork if you like, but I prefer to liberally sprinkle the sugar in a long line down the middle of my pancake, followed by a sprinkling of lemon juice and a pinch of zest, then I roll the pancake into a long sausage shape and eat, messily and greedily, with my sticky fingers.

VIRGIN PIÑA COLADA

*1½ cups
pineapple juice*

—

*½ cup coconut
milk*

—

*1 tbsp fresh
lime juice*

—

crushed ice

*To serve
(optional):*

*chunks of fresh
pineapple*

—

glacé cherries

—

cocktail sticks

—

*paper cocktail
umbrellas*

Difficulty ★ Time: ★

The only absolutely reliable hangover cure, according to some hardened drinkers, is to never stop. But, on the whole, that's seldom possible or, indeed, desirable: the modern scientific take on hair of the dog is that at some point the dog will turn round and give you a nip. That's why this is a "virgin" piña colada rather than the alcoholic version, which contains rum.

The best way to savor this drink is to imagine yourself sitting under the tropical shade of a palm or casuarina tree looking out over a white sand beach towards a shimmering, azure horizon; there's no better hangover cure than that. Hint: The secret is to close your eyes while you drink it, unless, of course, you really are sitting in a tropical paradise, in which case I recommend you open your eyes and go for a swim.

Milton's method ☞ Place all the ingredients in a blender. Give them a quick whiz for about 10 seconds and serve immediately in tall glasses. And, if you have cocktail sticks, chunks of fresh pineapple, glacé cherries and paper cocktail umbrellas, feel free to improvise a tacky decoration to stick in the top of your drink.

LEMON LASSI

2 tsp superfine
sugar
—
juice of 1 and
zest of ½
unwaxed lemon
—
2¼ cups plain
natural yogurt
—
¼ cup water
—
handful of finely
crushed ice
—
2 thin slices
lemon, for
serving

DIFFICULTY ★ TIME: ★

The lemon adds a bit of zing to this creamy drink, which is fantastically easy to make, though it does require a lot of yogurt. I like a thick consistency, so I add only a tiny amount of water and, rather than putting the ingredients in a blender, I mix them by hand in a bowl. I find this keeps the texture of the yogurt creamy and silky, whereas blending makes it thin and grainy.

Milton's method ☞ Mix the sugar and lemon juice in a small bowl and stir until the sugar is absorbed by the juice. Transfer to a larger bowl, add the remaining ingredients and mix thoroughly, but not violently, with a spatula.

Serve immediately in tall glasses and garnish each glass with a thin slice of lemon.

LIME SODA

4 limes

—

2 pinches salt

—

sparkling mineral water, chilled

—

ice (optional)

DIFFICULTY ★ TIME: ★

This is a popular street drink in India, where it makes a refreshing pick-me-up in the afternoon heat. Adding salt might seem strange but it's this ingredient that makes it such a supremely good rehydrating drink. Don't mess around with tumblers or Tom Collins glasses here—get out some pint glasses and properly relieve your thirst.

Milton's method ☞ Squeeze the juice from the limes into two pint-sized glasses, add a pinch of salt to each glass and top up with sparkling mineral water. Add ice, if you like.

Let us have

WINE
AND WOMEN,
mirth and laughter,

Sermons and soda water the day after.

Lord Byron

SUMMER BERRIES COMPOTE WITH GREEK YOGURT AND GRANOLA

For the summer berries compote:

18 oz mixed summer fruits
—
2 oz superfine sugar
—
2 tbsp water
—
2 tbsp lemon juice

For the granola:

1½ tbsp unsalted butter
—
1½ oz soft brown sugar
—
1 tbsp honey
—
8 oz large old-fashioned oats
—
1 oz crushed hazelnuts
—
2½ oz dried cranberries

To serve:

Greek yogurt

DIFFICULTY: ★★ TIME: ★★★★

This recipe somehow conspires to be both healthy-tasting and decadent—an ideal combination in my view. It's also a great union of textures: crunchy granola, creamy yogurt and soft fruits. I've given instructions for making the granola from scratch, but you can use shop-bought granola if you like. A cheat's way with the summer berries is to buy frozen fruits, which are readily available in supermarkets: a typical selection might include strawberries, raspberries, black currants, cherries, red currants and blackberries. Using frozen fruits means you can still eat this out of season.

Serve with Greek yogurt rather than the watered-down variety; it tastes much better.

Milton's method ☞ For the summer berries compote: Put the berries, sugar, water and lemon juice into a non-reactive saucepan and warm gently over low heat for about 10 minutes, stirring a couple of times until all the sugar has dissolved and the liquid has reduced slightly. Set aside to cool.

For the granola: Preheat the oven to 425°F. Melt the butter in a saucepan over a low heat. Add the sugar and honey and stir in until you have a beautiful-smelling, buttery syrup.

Add the oats, nuts and cranberries and stir thoroughly so that everything gets coated in the mixture. It will look a little dry, but that's fine.

Spread the mixture evenly in a greased baking tray and place in the hot oven. Cook for about 10 minutes but keep a careful eye on it as it burns easily. After about five minutes, take the tray out of the oven, give it a shake and then return it to the oven.

When the granola mixture is golden, but before it takes on a deeper shade of brown, remove it from the oven. Leave it to cool and get crispy and brittle, then break it up and store in an airtight container.

To serve: Spoon the summer berries compote into two bowls, add a couple of spoonfuls of Greek yogurt to each bowl and sprinkle with the granola.

THE KNICKERBOCKER
GLORY WITH REFRESHERS

½ packet vegetarian strawberry gelatin alternative or jelly crystals

—

4 ready-made meringue nests

—

1 packet Refreshers or other fruit-flavored fizzy candy

—

½ ripe mango, cut into ½-inch cubes

—

12 red grapes, halved

—

12 strawberries, hulled and halved

—

handful of blueberries

—

6 scoops vanilla ice cream

—

whipped cream from a can

—

4 praline wafers

DIFFICULTY: ★★   TIME: ★★★

Much of the fun of this absurd, multi-layered creation is in the making of it and the admiring of the surreal finished product—straight out of a children's birthday party. A dessert containing meringue, jelly, whipped cream and fruit-flavored fizzy sweets is clearly not for adults, at least not serious ones, but I invite you to revel in the joyful childishness of the Knickerbocker Glory: in fact, why not go the whole hog and finish it off with a lit sparkler?

Vegetarian jelly alternatives are now widely available and I prefer them to gelatin.

Milton's method ☞ Follow the packet instructions to make up the strawberry jelly; you will need about 1¼ cups. Allow to cool and set.

Once the jelly is set, take the meringue nests and half the Refreshers sweets and lightly bash them up in a bowl with the end of a rolling pin, until they are broken into coarse bits (not too fine).

Prepare the fruit, and start to assemble the dessert by mashing up the jelly and putting equal amounts in the bottom of two tall glasses (proper ice cream sundae glasses are best, but Tom Collins glasses, or similar, will do). Layer the fruit, ice cream and meringue mix on top of the jelly, and repeat until you get to the top of the glasses.

Squirt on some whipped cream, decorate with the remaining Refreshers and the wafers and serve immediately with long spoons for ease of eating. Feel free to add your own decorations in the way of paper umbrellas, sparklers and other ludicrous accoutrements.

Not many restaurants will serve the type of mouth-fizzing, toe-tingling, eye-popping food that you need to relieve your hangover symptoms, so it looks like you'll have to strap on your skates and zoom out (but mind the buses!).

It does depend on your locale, but most restaurants will be able to whip up an indulgent sundae. Or try a posh ice cream "soda" with a twist—prosecco with bellini ice cream, for example, or failing that, vanilla. Be prepared to spend some money while experimenting. And don't blame me if you end up spending a lot (see disclaimers at the back of this book).

If you're fortunate enough to have an ice-cream parlor on your doorstep this is the place to head to be bombarded by all manner of knickerbocker glories, floats, sundaes and sodas: absolutely ideal. You'll feel like a small child again but, most important, a small child who is having fun.

4

THE

ATOMIC

suspect that if you look in the mirror you might still see a mushroom cloud above your head, evidence of the explosion that has taken place inside you. As a consequence you feel damaged. Your head hurts. And it is as though your insides have been stripped out and there is almost nothing left. The bomb blast has left an enormous crater. For this reason, you are feeling monstrously hungry. You have no nausea, but an enormous appetite. This is a very physical hangover and there are few of what Kingsley Amis would call "metaphysical" aspects to it apart from the fact that you might feel more easily irritable than usual and perhaps a little jaded and leery of what life has to offer to you today. But there is none of the self-loathing associated with the Broken Compass. The best thing you can do, other than to replace the fluids you have lost, is to eat. A lot. Tuck in to these hearty recipes, which will repair some of the devastation that the booze has wrought.

CHORIZO OMELETTE

*3½ oz
good-quality
cooking chorizo,
finely sliced*

—

*olive oil,
for frying*

—

*¼ red onion,
diced*

—

*1 fresh ripe
tomato, diced*

—

*4 free-range
eggs, beaten
and lightly
seasoned with
salt and pepper*

—

*½ handful
fresh mint,
finely chopped*

—

*1 oz feta cheese
(optional)*

DIFFICULTY: ★★ TIME: ★★

Chorizo, as a breakfast ingredient, requires a little forethought: it is pungently garlicky, salty, spicy and rich, so eating too much of it may have the unintended effect of delaying your recovery rather than accelerating it. However, this omelette spares you the full force of the chorizo, while delivering enough of a kick to make it an invigorating and satisfying hungover breakfast.

Milton's method ☞ Heat a little olive oil in a frying pan over fairly high heat, then fry the slices of chorizo. After about three minutes, when the underside is brown-gold and bubbling, flip the chorizo over and cook for another three minutes or so. Add the onion and cook for a couple of minutes, stirring to ensure it does not burn. Add the tomato and cook for another two minutes.

Reduce the heat to medium. Combine the mint and eggs and pour the mixture into the pan, tilting to make sure the egg is evenly distributed. Shuffle the chorizo, onion and tomato around so the egg can reach everywhere in the pan.

Cook gently for about five minutes, lifting the omelette slightly with a spatula so any liquid egg can run underneath and start to set. Once the egg has almost set, crumble the feta, if using, on top. Fold one half of the omelette over the other to make a semi-circle. Tip the omelette onto a plate, cut in half and serve with thick slices of bread and butter.

THE BREAKFAST BURGER

*1 onion,
roughly chopped*

—

1 tbsp ketchup

—

*2 tsp
Worcestershire
sauce*

—

*½ tsp sweet
paprika*

—

*¾ lb free-range
seasoned
sausage meat*

—

1 egg yolk

—

2 tsp dried sage

—

*handful of finely
chopped chives*

—

*freshly ground
black pepper*

—

*4 English
muffins,
cut in half*

DIFFICULTY: ★★★ TIME: ★★

In the tradition of the British breakfast this burger uses pork sausage meat rather than minced beef, which is arguably a little heavy for the first meal of the day (indeed, some might argue that the entire concept of a burger is too heavy, though I heartily disagree). The consistency of sausage meat makes it ideal for shaping into burgers, and you don't need to add any butter or oil to cook them—there's plenty of fat in the meat. I ask my butcher for sausage meat from outdoor-bred pigs, which I prefer to meat from pigs that have never seen sunlight.

I've allowed two smallish burgers per person, squeezed into lightly toasted English muffins. You may want to add a fried egg to each muffin or, for the true carnivore, a piece of grilled bacon.

Milton's method ☞ Blend together the onion, ketchup, Worcestershire sauce and paprika in a food processor.

In a large bowl combine the onion mixture with the sausage meat, egg yolk, sage, chives and black pepper. Use some muscle to mix all the ingredients thoroughly with a wooden spoon.

With wet hands, make four even-sized balls out of the mixture and then flatten each one to form a patty shape. Put on a covered plate in the fridge for 45 minutes.

Heat a non-stick frying pan over medium high heat and put the burgers into it without any additional fat. Cook them for about five minutes on one side, then reduce the heat a little, flip the burgers over and cook for five minutes on the other side. Flip them over again and cook for another three minutes per side on a low to medium heat, until cooked through.

While the burgers are cooking, lightly toast the muffins under the broiler.

Serve each burger in a toasted muffin with condiments of your choice, mustard and ketchup being the obvious ones.

CARDAMOM PORRIDGE
WITH SPICY APPLE SAUCE

For the spicy apple sauce:

18 oz cooking apples (such as Gala), peeled, cored and chopped

—

¼ cup superfine sugar

—

¼ cup raisins

—

⅔ cup water

—

3 star anise

—

3 cloves

—

2 small cinnamon sticks

—

½ tsp ground cinnamon

—

½ tsp allspice

—

1 tsp grated fresh ginger

—

1 tbsp unsalted butter

DIFFICULTY: ★★ TIME: ★★

I was never a fan of porridge, finding it stodgy and boring—and with a hangover, its texture was particularly unappealing. But on a recent trek through the Himalayas I realized that the main benefit of porridge is the incredible amount of slow-burning energy it provides—and its value should not be underestimated by the hangover sufferer any less than by the high-altitude trekker.

So, after I returned to England's dull, gray shores, I set about creating a porridge that I could actually enjoy and that was both healthy and filling. This is it: a concoction that is at once creamy, fruity, spicy, sweet and tart, and will give you energy for hours.

Milton's method ☞ Put the chopped apple, sugar, raisins, water and spices in a non-reactive saucepan, cover with a lid, and cook gently for about 20 minutes.

Take the lid off and, using a wooden spoon, stir the apples, which should now be mushy, so that they begin to break up. You will need to do this for a little while to make a fairly smooth apple sauce, though it's preferable to keep a little texture, rather than end up with a purée. Keep the sauce warm on a very low heat while you prepare the porridge.

For the porridge:

5 oz porridge oats

—

1¾ cup whole or 2% milk

—

3 cardamom pods, lightly crushed and left whole

—

1 tbsp soft brown sugar, to serve

Put the oats, milk and cardamom pods into a separate saucepan and slowly bring to the boil. Simmer for about six minutes until the porridge has a creamy consistency and the oats are fully softened.

Add the butter to the apple sauce and stir in until it has melted.

Spoon half the apple sauce into the porridge and stir well. Pick out with a metal spoon as many of the whole spices as you can see before serving.

Pour the porridge in bowls, and top each bowl with a large spoonful of the apple sauce. Sprinkle the soft brown sugar over the surface and serve as soon as it has melted into the mixture. Watch out for any cloves and star anise lurking in the porridge!

POTATO HASH WITH AVOCADO AND BACON

about 1 lb old white potatoes, peeled and roughly cubed

—

olive oil, for frying

—

4 slices free-range bacon (smoked or unsmoked)

—

1 onion, cut into large rough dice

—

½ tsp sweet paprika

—

splash of Worcestershire sauce

—

salt and pepper

—

few drops of Tabasco sauce, to taste

—

1 ripe avocado, peeled, cored and thinly sliced

DIFFICULTY: ★★ TIME: ★★

I first had this breakfast—or something similar to it—at a cafe in some back street in Brighton, on New Year's Day a few years ago, after a night's hard partying and almost no sleep. My memories of that breakfast are hazy, but I remember that I liked it a lot and ate all of it. I more distinctly remember fearing cardiac arrest as I humped up the hill to the railway station afterwards.

The recipe I've given here is consistent with my memory, if not the reality, of the breakfast I ate that morning. It is super-simple but it's possible to customize it, too, by adding a red pepper into the hash, for example, or by placing a poached egg on top or crumbling some cheese over the hot potato hash. Experimenting with food is fun and this recipe (which I often cook for breakfast, lunch or dinner) is particularly ideal for playing around with.

For the vinaigrette:

4 tbsp extra-virgin olive oil
—
1 tbsp balsamic vinegar

Milton's method ☞ Wash and boil the potatoes for about 10 minutes in cold salted water, until they are softened slightly but still firm. Drain the potatoes and allow them to dry.

Heat a good glug of olive oil in a frying pan and, when it begins to smoke, add the drained potatoes. Fry the potatoes on all sides until they are golden and crispy.

In the meantime, grill the bacon, and combine the oil and vinegar, either in a bowl by stirring vigorously, or in a jam jar or other container that you can seal and shake until they are well mixed.

Add the onion to the potatoes and stir thoroughly. Cook and stir for a couple of minutes, then add the paprika and the Worcestershire sauce, and season well with salt and pepper.

Fry for a few more minutes until the onion has begun to color, taking care not to let the potato burn, then pile the hash in mounds on two plates. Sprinkle with a few drops of Tabasco sauce, fan the avocado slices on top of each potato mound, then top with the bacon rashers and spoon a few teaspoons of vinaigrette over each portion.

Serve immediately.

CHEESE, RED ONION AND CHUTNEY TOASTIES

4 square, fairly thin slices bread

—

butter, to taste

—

3½ oz aged cheddar cheese, thinly sliced

—

½ red onion, thinly sliced

—

2 heaped tsp spicy mango chutney

DIFFICULTY: ★★ TIME: ★★

The word "toastie" is evocative of comfort and warmth (mental as well as physical), something that hangover sufferers often crave. So I need no further excuse for introducing you to the delights of this cheese, red onion and chutney toastie, which is guaranteed to bring warmth flooding back into your life.

I discovered this for myself one New Year's Day, after following Ernest Hemingway's edict: "Always do sober what you said you'd do drunk. That will teach you to keep your mouth shut." For me, this involved swimming in an ice-cold Welsh river with a monumental hangover after boasting the night before that I could swim anywhere in the world. After narrowly avoiding cardiac arrest and hypothermia, I made it back to the snug cottage where I was staying, and rustled up these little hot triangles of joy.

This toastie is best made in a toasted-sandwich maker, so that you get a nicely sealed sandwich with a deliciously gooey cheese, onion and chutney mix inside. It's also best to use ready-sliced bread and a spicy mango chutney rather than the regular version. If you don't have a sandwich maker, you can fry or grill your sandwich instead.

Milton's method ☞ If you're using a sandwich maker, switch it on to heat up.

Butter each slice of bread on one side only.

Layer the slices of cheese and onion on the unbuttered side of two slices of bread, then slap on the chutney, spreading it as evenly as you can.

Top each sandwich with a second slice of bread, buttered-side up.

Put a little butter into the bottom half of the sandwich maker, wait for it to melt, then whack in one of the sandwiches and clamp down the lid. Show no mercy—the bread needs to get properly crimped.

Wait for the sandwich maker to do its business, about five minutes, then remove the toasted sandwich to a plate, using a wooden or plastic spatula. Now whack in the second sandwich.

Cut the sandwiches into triangles and serve immediately, either on their own or with a little crisp green salad and some mayonnaise (for dipping your sandwich into as you eat it with your fingers). Be careful: The filling gets very hot.

SPICY SAUSAGE AND BEAN CASSEROLE

olive oil,
for frying
—
1 onion, diced
—
6 merguez
sausages,
each cut into
2-inch pieces
—
2 garlic cloves,
minced
—
½ tsp cayenne
pepper
—
½ vegetable
stock cube
—
¾ cup red wine
—
1 14-oz can
chopped tomatoes
—
1 tbsp tomato
purée
—
¼ cup water
—
pinch of sugar
—
black pepper
—
salt

DIFFICULTY: ★★★ TIME: ★★★

This is a reworking of another British breakfast favorite—sausage and beans. Instead of pork sausages, though, I've used merguez—a spicy North African sausage usually made with lamb—and substituted borlotti beans for baked beans. It's all done in the same pan, so it's nice and easy and there's less washing up afterwards. I find this dish tastes best the following day, as the sauce gets richer and thicker when left overnight. So either make it in advance on a night when you know there's a good chance you'll want it the following morning, or just make some extra in the morning and have it two days in a row.

The first time I made this was in Brittany, when I served it with a fried egg on top, a massive hunk of smelly ripe Camembert on the side and half a fresh baguette straight from the boulangerie. The red wine I used was discovered, uncorked, in front of the still-smoking fire, left over from the previous night's session. This kind of egregious self-indulgence is the trademark of a good hungover breakfast. I'll leave the choice of extras up to you, but I consider the baguette essential for mopping up all the delicious sauce.

freshly ground black pepper

—

generous splash (about 1 tsp) of Worcestershire sauce

—

1 7-oz can borlotti beans, drained

—

handful of roughly chopped flat-leaf parsley

—

2 fresh baguettes, for serving

Milton's method ☞ In a heavy metal casserole with a lid, heat a little oil over medium heat and chuck in the onion, making sure it gets coated with oil. Partially cover with the lid and leave the onion to cook for a few minutes, stirring once or twice, until it's softened and started to turn golden.

Add the sausages and the garlic and cook for about five minutes, stirring occasionally, until the sausages begin to brown.

Add the cayenne pepper and crumble half a stock cube into the casserole. Stir, then pour in the wine.

Bring to the boil and reduce the sauce for about four minutes (all the alcohol will also evaporate).

Stir in the tomatoes, tomato purée and water, then add a pinch of sugar to balance the spice, along with some freshly ground black pepper and a splash of Worcestershire sauce.

Bring to the boil and simmer for two minutes, stirring a couple of times, then turn the heat down, add the beans, cover and cook gently for about 20 minutes, stirring occasionally to ensure the sauce doesn't stick to the bottom.

Add a little extra seasoning to taste, cook for a further minute then stir in the chopped parsley, remove from the heat and leave to stand for five minutes with the lid on. Serve hot, with a baguette on the side of each plate.

TAGLIATELLE ALLA CARBONARA

8 oz dried
tagliatelle
—
olive oil, for
frying
—
3½ oz streaky
free-range
smoked bacon or
pancetta, cut into
1-inch strips
—
½ onion, thinly
sliced
—
2 garlic cloves,
minced
—
2 free-range
eggs, beaten
—
2 oz freshly
grated parmesan
—
salt and pepper
—
generous handful
of flat-leaf
parsley, roughly
chopped

DIFFICULTY: ★★ TIME: ★★

An Italian friend of mine was in a Berlin cafe one morning when he spotted something on the menu he thought he might fancy—an Italian breakfast. "What's the Italian breakfast?" he asked the waiter. "An espresso and a cigarette" came the reply.

I could have included it as a recipe in this book, but that would have been a little lazy of me. Instead, here's another Italian favorite that might come as a surprise on a breakfast or brunch menu, but if you consider that it's basically scrambled egg and bacon with pasta, it makes more sense. The pasta, with its mass of carbohydrate, is ideal for the Atomic hangover when you want to fill up on food, and the slow release of energy from the pasta will keep you going for much of the day. I also like to have some bread on the side to mop up the sauce.

There's no cream in this recipe, as this, I've been told by my Italian friend, is an utterly British adulteration of carbonara: the creaminess comes instead from the combination of egg and cheese.

Milton's method ☞ Cook the tagliatelle in a saucepan of boiling, salted water according to the instructions. Take care not to overcook it; you want it al dente.

While the pasta is cooking, heat a little oil in a heavy metal casserole (or a large saucepan) and cook the bacon over fairly high heat until it starts to turn golden and crispy.

Immediately add the onion and cook for a further three to four minutes, stirring occasionally to make sure that bacon and the onion don't burn.

Stir in the garlic and cook for a further two minutes.

Drain the tagliatelle—incompletely—in a colander; in other words, don't shake the colander too much, so that the pasta remains slightly wet.

Reduce the heat to medium and tip the tagliatelle into the bacon pan. Stir thoroughly so that the bacon, onion and garlic combine well with the pasta.

Add the beaten eggs, the cheese and salt and pepper to taste, and mix well. Cook for a couple of minutes until the eggs begin to set, then throw in the parsley, give a final stir, and serve immediately with some crusty bread on the side.

THE ENGLISH BREAKFAST TORTILLA

3 medium-sized
old potatoes,
peeled and cut
into thin slices
—
olive oil, for frying
—
3½ oz streaky
bacon/pancetta
—
4 free-range
pork chipolata
sausages, each
cut into 3 pieces
—
handful of cup
mushrooms,
sliced
—
½ onion, finely
diced
—
½ red sweet
pepper, de-seeded
and cut into
2-inch strips
—
pinch of sweet
paprika
—
1 tbsp chopped
fresh thyme
(optional)
—
6 medium-sized
free-range eggs,
lightly beaten
and seasoned
—
salt and pepper

DIFFICULTY: ★★★ TIME: ★★

This is exactly what it says: the essential ingredients of a traditional English breakfast (sausage, bacon, egg and mushrooms), cooked in a single pan, with the end result resembling something like a Spanish tortilla. It's an epic breakfast (have it late morning and you're unlikely to feel hungry again until evening) and, being cooked in a single pan, it won't create as much washing up as the conventional English breakfast.

Milton's method ☞ Wash and boil the sliced potatoes in salted water for about four minutes until they are slightly softened but still firm. Drain them and set aside.

In a medium-sized, non-stick, ovenproof frying pan (no plastic handle!) heat a little oil, and fry the bacon and sausages over medium-high heat for about six or seven minutes, stirring occasionally, until the ingredients begin to turn crispy and take on a golden brown color.

Add the mushrooms, along with the potatoes, stirring them in carefully so that the potatoes don't break up. Fry for another four minutes or so, until the potatoes start to golden.

Add the onion, fry for a couple more minutes and then add the sweet pepper, sweet paprika and thyme leaves. Season to taste with salt and pepper. Let everything cook for another two minutes, stirring to prevent burning.

Make sure the ingredients are evenly distributed, then reduce the heat to low-medium and pour in the eggs, tilting the pan and moving the ingredients around gently with a wooden spoon so the egg mixture reaches all corners of the pan. Leave it to cook gently for about six minutes or until the egg in contact with the base of the pan has set (you should then be able lift the tortilla away from the sides of the pan and slide it around).

Put the pan in a pre-heated broiler for five minutes until the egg on top has set.

Cut in half and serve with buttered toast and condiments of your choice; I like to have a couple of pickled chilis with this.

If you're not quite up to cooking for yourself the hearty meal that you so evidently need, then I suggest you head to a British pub—dangerous territory, perhaps—for a savory meat pie. A pie is exactly the kind of food that most people won't want to cook when they are hungover, particularly if it involves making pastry from scratch.

Most British pubs, though, will serve some sort of pastry concoction that will keep the hunger away for a few hours and may even persuade you that more alcohol is in order (please see disclaimers absolving this author of all responsibility for your mental and physical well-being). Have mashed potato with your pie in order to fulfil your stodge quotient. Some authors might recommend a mixed grill for this type of hangover, but in my experience overindulgence in meat (particularly that of dubious quality) can be, for all kinds of reasons, a serious mistake.

5

You feel as though someone has ripped your head off and thrown a cement mixer inside you before sealing you up again. Your insides feel as though they're being twisted inside-out and turned around and around. There's a guy down there, standing next to the cement mixer, with thick forearms, a sunburned neck, a high-viz jacket and a cigarette hanging out of his mouth, shovelling spadefuls of sand inside you. It goes without saying that you don't feel well. I mean, who would under these circumstances? But the terrible thing is that it actually appears to be getting worse. The mixer is slowly migrating up to your head, being pushed by that guy in the jacket, who has now stubbed out a number of cigarettes and has just lit his latest. You need to kill the little builder guy and turn that cement mixer off. Immediately. But how to do it? Well, to start with, I suggest that you eat something to soothe your stomach and make the world stand still again. Try something from this gentle menu of comforting treats.

A TURKISH BREAKFAST

4 free-range
eggs
—
salt and pepper
—
extra-virgin
olive oil,
for drizzling
—
5 oz feta cheese
—
1–2 tsp dried
oregano,
or to taste
—
clear honey
—
unsalted butter,
softened (for
spreading on
bread)
—
handful of good
black olives
—
2 good-quality
sweet
Mediterranean
tomatoes, sliced
—
Turkish bread
—
black tea

DIFFICULTY: ★ TIME: ★★

Apart from boiling some eggs, there's no cooking involved in creating this Turkish-style breakfast; it's more an assembly of choice ingredients, principally eggs, cheese, olives, tomatoes, bread and honey. Everything is readily available, except perhaps for truly authentic Turkish bread. If you don't have a Turkish grocer nearby, then fresh white bread with sesame seeds will give a reasonable approximation.

Milton's method ☞ Boil the eggs to your liking; hard-boiled is the usual preference with a Turkish breakfast.

If you have hard-boiled your eggs, peel them and cut in quarters, then put on two plates, season with salt and pepper and drizzle a little oil over them.

Cut the feta cheese into slices, arrange on the plates, sprinkle with oregano and drizzle with a little more oil.

Spoon some honey into two small ramekins and put them on the plates. Do the same with some softened butter.

Arrange the olives and the tomatoes on the plates and serve with the bread and some light, slightly sweetened black tea.

FRENCH TOAST WITH BANANA COMPOTE

For the banana compote:

½ cup orange juice

—

juice of 1 lemon

—

2 tbsp runny honey

—

2 tbsp soft brown sugar

—

seeds from 2 cardamom pods

—

2 tbsp unsalted butter

—

2 large bananas, sliced

—

1 tbsp dark rum

DIFFICULTY: ★★ TIME: ★★

When I was in Vietnam, my French-Canadian host was offended when I described his French toast as 'eggy-bread'; he told me that it did not do justice to its "golden loveliness." So let's call it French toast, shall we?

There is an infinite number of variations on French toast, but I've given you the most basic, non-sugary version, with a sweet banana compote on the side spiced up with a little rum and cardamom.

Milton's method ☞ For the banana compote: In a non-reactive saucepan, combine the orange and lemon juices and gently simmer over low heat for 10 minutes until the mixture has reduced slightly.

Add the honey, brown sugar and cardamom seeds. Stir until the sugar has dissolved.

Remove from the heat and whisk in the butter. Leave to cool slightly, then add the sliced banana and the rum. Place the compote back on a very low heat to keep warm, but *don't let it boil,* while you make the French toast.

For the French toast: Place the beaten eggs in a shallow bowl and stir in the milk and cinnamon.

Dip each piece of bread in turn in the egg mixture so that both sides get covered, but don't allow the bread to soak up too much egg or it will disintegrate. Carefully place each piece of bread to one side, but don't stack them on top of one another.

Melt a little butter in a frying pan over medium-high heat; when the butter has melted, add the bread to the pan (you may have to do this two pieces at a time and add a little more butter for the next batch). Check the bottom of the bread, using a slice to lift it up, to make sure it doesn't burn, and when it has acquired its characteristic "golden loveliness," flip the bread over and cook on the other side.

Serve the hot toast with the banana compote in small bowls on the side for dipping in or spooning on to the toast.

MILTON CRAWFORD'S FISH FINGER SANDWICH

(with garlic green pea mayo)

8 frozen fish fingers (or homemade ones, see below)

—

4 large slices thick white bread

For the homemade fish fingers:

9 oz firm white fish fillet, skinned

—

1 oz flour, seasoned with a little salt and pepper

—

2 free-range eggs, beaten

—

2 oz fine fresh bread crumbs

—

vegetable oil, for frying

DIFFICULTY: ★★ / ★★★★ * TIME: ★★

White fish is good for settling an upset stomach and the fish finger sandwich—a childhood favorite—is classic comfort food. Admittedly, fish that has been coated in egg and bread crumbs may not have the same soothing effect as boiled or steamed fish, but personal experience has revealed that fish fingers can nonetheless have a beneficial impact on a hungover tummy. For this sandwich, you can use either frozen fish fingers or homemade ones. I buy frozen fish fingers that come from sustainable fishing stocks, which are now widely available. However, I've also given instructions for making your own fish fingers, or "goujons," as you might find them described in some cookbooks and restaurant menus. But a "goujon sandwich" doesn't quite do it for me (and imagine what the French would say).

I wanted to have mushy peas with this dish but they're a bit too sloppy to sit happily in a sandwich, so I invented this garlic green pea mayo to which the cider vinegar adds a nice sharpness.

Milton's method ☞ For the fish fingers: If using frozen fish fingers, grill them according to the packet instructions. If making your own, cut the fish fillet into eight fish-finger-sized strips. Place the flour, eggs and bread crumbs in three separate shallow bowls. Coat each piece of fish first in the seasoned flour, then dip in the beaten egg and finally, roll in the bread crumbs, making sure that the bread crumbs are evenly coated across the fish.

---

* two stars denotes shop-bought fish fingers / four stars denotes homemade fish fingers

For the garlic green pea mayo:

1½ tbsp unsalted butter

—

1 garlic clove, minced

—

2½ oz frozen green peas

—

½ cup boiling water, from a kettle

—

3 tsp mayonnaise, from a jar

—

2 tsp cider vinegar

To serve:

squeeze of lemon juice

—

ketchup

—

Tabasco sauce

Heat some oil in a deep-fat fryer or a wok. When it's very hot, drop in the fish fingers, three or four at a time, and cook them for about one minute until golden and crispy. Remove them from the pan with a slotted spoon, to drain them, and then place on paper towels to soak up the excess oil.

For the garlic green pea mayo: Melt half the butter in a small, heavy saucepan over a medium heat. Add the garlic and stir for a couple of minutes, making sure that the garlic doesn't color.

Add the peas and stir a couple of times, then add the boiling water. Put a lid on the saucepan, bring to the boil and let boil for a couple of minutes, until the peas are tender.

Drain the peas and put them in a blender along with the remaining butter and the mayonnaise and vinegar. Season to taste and blend everything together until you have a fairly smooth purée.

To serve: Spread the green pea mayo on two slices of bread and lay the fish fingers on top. Squeeze a little lemon juice and some ketchup over them and sprinkle with Tabasco, to taste, then top each sandwich with a second slice of bread. Cut in half and serve immediately.

SWEET LASSI

handful of
ice cubes

—

1½ cups natural
yogurt

—

½ cup cold
water

—

pinch of
ground salt

—

4 tsp superfine
sugar

—

3 cardamom
pods

DIFFICULTY: ★ TIME: ★

This north Indian-style sweet lassi contains
cardamom, a spice that is often used in India to
treat flatulence—particularly useful, in my
experience, after an evening of ale or cider drinking.
It's also a good breath freshener, which can be
handy on a hungover morning.

The secret to making a good lassi is not to put
the ingredients in the blender but to mix them
together by hand in a bowl so that the lassi retains
a thick, silky yogurt texture.

This is a traditional recipe that also includes a
pinch of salt.

Milton's method ☞ Crush the ice, either in a blender
or by placing it in a clean kitchen towel and
bashing it with a rolling pin or pestle.

Gently stir together the yogurt, water, salt,
sugar and crushed ice in a large bowl with a wooden
spoon or spatula until the sugar and salt have
completely dissolved.

Roughly grind the cardamom pods with a mortar
and pestle and add the grainy, aromatic powder to
the yogurt mixture. Reserve a little for the garnish.

Serve in glasses and garnish the top of each drink
with the reserved cardamom.

Always do sober
what you said you'd do drunk.
That will teach you to keep

your mouth

sHUT.

Ernest Hemingway

THE PERFECT TEA
AND TOAST

1 packet
bread mix
—
½ stick softened
butter (get it
out of the fridge
an hour in
advance)
—
good-quality
traditional
thick-cut orange
marmalade
—
English breakfast
tea (Earl Grey,
Assam, etc., are
also acceptable)

DIFFICULTY: ★ TIME: ★★★★

When it feels like chaos has been unleashed upon
the world, or your part of it at least, then something
comfortingly familiar and normal is required to
give you some stability. In Britain, the first thing
that happens after some terrible news, or when
someone has fallen off their bicycle, is that somebody
will make a cup of tea. With a hangover, though,
tea *and* toast is the answer—the staple breakfast
diet of the time-pressed Brit.

Now, I admit that this is more of an idea than
a recipe, but the principles that underpin it are
Attention to Detail and Quality of Execution. Sadly,
tea and toast is too often a rushed afterthought of
a breakfast that isn't even consumed while sitting
down. But, to make it the soothing pleasure that it
ought to be, some care is required. This is what I
recommend you do to create the ultimate tea and
toast experience.

The most comforting, homely smell in the world,
to me at least, is that of freshly baked bread, and
there are a number of ways to achieve it. The first,
and most obvious, is to bake your own. This may
sound like a time-consuming and laborious
process, particularly with a hangover. However, you
can buy a ready-made bread mix (from almost any
supermarket and many small grocery stores) and
turn it into delicious bread within an hour and a
half. The other (rather half-baked) options are to
buy some fresh bread, or to get some old bread and
warm it up in the oven on a fairly low heat (though
it won't quite smell the same).

When it comes to making tea, don't just throw a tea bag in a mug: get the crockery out, make a pot of tea, put the milk in a jug, the sugar in a bowl. Listen: We at least pretend to be civilized people; and the very fact that you feel grubby and unevolved today is the best possible reason to lay on the civilization stuff extra thick.

So, dress up in something smart and clean. Get some traditional thick-cut orange marmalade and some proper butter; not the stuff you buy in a plastic tub. Put the butter in a butter tray and adorn with a butter knife. Get out the silver and your finest plates. Toast your homemade bread and pop it in a rack. Sit at the table with a clean tablecloth, elegant place mats, stiff linen napkins and a vase of bright, freshly cut seasonal flowers. Inhale the aroma of freshly baked bread and flowers, drink tea out of a cup, thickly butter your toast, then slather on the marmalade with your silver knife and admire just how civilized you are.

Milton's method ☞ Make your bread. Make the tea. Toast your bread. Serve the toast, in a rack, with butter, marmalade and tea in their appropriate receptacles. Eat, chat, read a newspaper and relax.

SWISS RÖSTI AND POACHED EGGS

1¼ lb white potatoes (about 4 medium to large spuds)

—

2 garlic cloves, finely minced

—

salt and black pepper

—

1½ tbsp unsalted butter

—

glug of olive oil

—

4 free-range eggs

—

1 tsp white wine vinegar, for poaching eggs

DIFFICULTY: ★★   TIME: ★★★★★

Potatoes are, without doubt, my favorite vegetable. You can keep your squashes and artichokes, your fennel and snow peas, your kohlrabi and endive just as long as I have my potatoes. After all, according to A. A. Milne, "If a fellow really likes *potatoes*, he must be a pretty decent sort of fellow."

But what's so good about potatoes? In a word: versatility. Once you think you know every way that you can cook a potato, another one comes along, and the Swiss rösti stretches the possibilities of the mighty tuber even further. I fell in love with its great blend of 'tato textures: crispy on the inside, creamy in the middle, it makes an ideal hungover breakfast with poached eggs on top.

The best way to prepare the potatoes is to boil them in their skins the night before and place them, unpeeled, in an airtight container in the fridge, for use up to 24 hours later. But if you haven't been able to organize this, just leave them to cool down for at least 30 minutes before grating them.

A word of warning: watch those shaky hands with wobbly poached eggs!

Milton's method ☞ Scrub the potatoes and place them, with their skins still on, in a large pan filled with cold, salted water. Bring to a boil and cook for about 10 minutes (they should become slightly more tender but remain firm), then drain and allow them to cool for at least 30 minutes.

Peel the potatoes, then coarsely grate them into a bowl with a hand grater, adding plenty of seasoning and the minced cloves of garlic. Make sure the garlic and seasoning are evenly distributed.

Melt the butter and olive oil in a large, non-stick frying pan. When the pan is hot, add the potato. Cook for five minutes over fairly high heat. When the underside begins to turn golden, flip the mixture over (it won't stick together at this stage), then, using a metal slice, divide it into four roughly circular "cakes," about an inch deep, in the pan.

Press each "cake" down slightly with the slice and cook for a further five minutes on high heat, then flip them over (the potato should now be sticking together) and turn down the heat to low-medium. Cook gently for another 10 minutes on each side, checking occasionally to make sure that the potato does not burn.

About five minutes before your rösti is ready, heat some salted water in a saucepan with the vinegar, for poaching the eggs. The temperature is right when there are little bubbles slowly rising to the surface; the water should not be boiling vigorously. Break the eggs into the water and cook on low to medium heat for 4–5 minutes for a soft-poached egg.

Divide the rösti between two plates. Drain the eggs using a slotted spoon, rinse under a little cold water, then drain once more, and place an egg on each rösti. Season with salt and freshly ground pepper and serve.

BANANA AND PASSION FRUIT SMOOTHIE

3 passion fruit

—

2 very ripe soft bananas, roughly chopped

—

2 tsp runny honey

—

1¼ cup natural yogurt

—

1 cup ice cubes

DIFFICULTY: ★ TIME: ★

This smoothie is a great stomach-soother, although it's not the bland recipe you might expect from such a remedy, as the passion fruit adds a delicious tropical sharpness. Some people prefer to sieve the passion fruit pulp in order to get rid of the seeds, but I like the texture they give to the smoothie; the little black dots are like exotic punctuation in a smoothie sentence.

Making this is as simple as falling off the pavement (yes, you remember that, do you?).

Milton's method ☞ Cut the passion fruit in half and scoop out the flesh and seeds with a teaspoon. Reserve half the pulp from one of the passion fruits for the garnish.

Put the remaining pulp and all the other ingredients in a blender, and pulse until the ice has been broken down.

Serve in glasses and spoon the reserved passion fruit pulp on top.

The easiest takeout of all to organize, or at least the most readily available, is the ubiquitous pizza. And a doughy Italian bicycle wheel is the ideal food to put the brakes on the churning in your stomach until it finally stops. The obvious thing to point out here is that you shouldn't go for a silly topping. By that, I mean anything that will further upset your stomach, particularly spicy and fatty processed meats. Depending on your attitude toward cheese you may also want to keep this to a minimum, though I personally can never get enough of the stuff—a four-cheese quattro formaggi would suit me fine.

A particularly plain version of the "Neapolitan pancake," which also seems fairly healthy, is spinach with ricotta cheese. And the other option is to get the plainest pizza you can and add your own toppings. Spinach with egg is a nice one for breakfast: just crack the eggs on top of the pizza and stick it in the oven for five minutes.

6

This hangover is greatly feared, as it represents the very nadir of the hungover state, the dark immobile sludge at the bottom of a vast sewer. It combines both acute physical and psychological symptoms. It is a living nightmare. Indeed, it could also be called "Apocalypse Now," as its intensity is such that you feel you could be a doomed figure in an Hieronymus Bosch painting or, indeed, the living embodiment of one of Francis Bacon's distorted portraits. Without wanting to state the obvious, you drank too much. You may have any number of the following: nausea; a swimming, aching head; cold sweats; trembling hands; shivering; coughing; prickly eyes; and stabbing pain across your body. In between the pain and the fever, there are nightmarish visions of what might have happened last night, things that you're not quite aware are true or not. You have terrible pangs of guilt. Moments of existential clarity and a sense of really getting to the bottom of your "self" are mixed with a general sense of doom and futility. These, you might feel, are the end times for you: either the world is about to end or your own continued participation in it seems at best tenuous. But I'd recommend having breakfast first. You may not feel like it. You may doubt that it is even possible for you to eat. However, these exceptionally clean recipes of healthy food should help to banish the nausea, restore your pulse and ease the cold sweats. And if you really can't face it, then perhaps lots of rest and plenty of water is the only cure for you.

MELON, FETA, MINT AND HAM SALAD

1 small ripe cantaloupe, cut into cubes

—

3½ oz feta cheese, cut into cubes

—

½ small red onion, very finely diced

—

small handful of fresh mint, finely chopped

—

1 tbsp good-quality balsamic vinegar, plus extra for drizzling

—

salt and pepper

—

4 thin slices Parma or serrano ham

—

2 sprigs fresh mint (optional)

DIFFICULTY: ★ TIME: ★

If you can get outdoors for some fresh air and sunshine you should start to feel better immediately. Of course, that might not be as easy as it sounds, depending on your physical state. One hungover morning in a friend's house, I remember singing a song inspired by my inability to move, invented in a kind of frenzied, sofa-bound semi-delirium, which went something like this:

My legs are like je-huh-lly: they have no bones
My legs are like je-huh-lly: they have no bones
Please send for a taxi and find me my phone

This wasn't an occasion when I was able to go outdoors and sit in a beautiful garden. But if it's sunny and warm and you can sit outside, then you might want to prepare this very simple dish, which is fresh, fruity and salty and tastes best when you eat it in the sun.

Milton's method ☞ Put the melon, feta cheese, onion, mint, balsamic vinegar and seasoning in a bowl and gently mix the ingredients.

Arrange the salad on two plates, in a tasteful mound, and artfully tear the ham over the top. If your Gremlin Boogie hangover is mild enough to still have any real aesthetic sense, you may want to drizzle a little balsamic vinegar over the top and garnish with a sprig of fresh mint.

CHEAT'S SMOKED SALMON EGGS BENEDICT

4 medium
free-range eggs
—
pinch of salt
—
1 tsp white wine
vinegar
—
2 English
muffins
—
small handful
of fresh chives,
finely chopped
(reserve 8 whole
chives for
garnishing)
—
5 oz crème
fraîche
—
freshly ground
black pepper
—
butter, for
spreading on
the muffins
—
3½ oz smoked
salmon
—
juice of ½
lemon
—
1 tbsp extra-
virgin olive
oil

DIFFICULTY: ★★ TIME: ★★

This variation on eggs Benedict, which uses smoked salmon rather than ham or bacon, is often called eggs royale, though my version is, strictly speaking, a bit of a cheat because of the lack of hollandaise sauce, which I find difficult to make and slightly unappealing due to its gloopy consistency and similarity in appearance and texture to custard. So this is a simple alternative that I find fresher, cleaner and tastier, though also less buttery and indulgent, than the original recipe.

The origin of eggs Benedict is disputed, but the story I like the best is the one involving a hungover man on a mission to find the exact combination of food to suit his jaded palate. His name, so the story goes, was Lemuel Benedict and he walked into the Waldorf Hotel in New York one morning in 1894 and, completely ignoring the menu, asked for buttered toast, poached eggs, crispy bacon and hollandaise sauce. The maître d' later substituted muffins for toast and ham for bacon and named the breakfast "eggs Benedict."

Anyhow, my version (eggs Crawford?) has neither ham nor hollandaise sauce, which makes the connection with the original dish suddenly seem rather tenuous. Anyhow, here it is:
Eggs Crawford à la Waldorf, sans Hollandaise.

Milton's method ☞ Heat a pan of salted water with a teaspoon of vinegar. When little bubbles start to slowly rise to the surface (the water should not be boiling vigorously), break the eggs into the water and cook them over low to medium heat for about 4–5 minutes for soft-poached eggs.

Cut the muffins in half and lightly toast.

Stir the chopped chives into the crème fraîche and season with a little black pepper.

Butter the muffins and dollop on a generous spoonful of the crème fraîche mixture.

Remove the eggs, using a slotted spoon, then rinse lightly in cold water and quickly and carefully drain on the spoon.

Layer a slice of smoked salmon on each muffin half, and lightly press it down to make a stable base for the eggs.

Balance an egg on top of each muffin, add a squeeze of lemon juice, lightly drizzle with olive oil and season with a little salt and pepper. Garnish with the whole chives and serve immediately.

TAHINI AND TOMATO TOAST

*4 slices brown
or multi-grain
bread
—
2 tbsp tahini
paste
—
4 good-quality
ripe tomatoes,
thinly sliced
—
4 tsp soy sauce
—
handful of
chopped flat-leaf
parsley,
to garnish*

Difficulty: ★   Time: ★

My friend and neighbor Jimmy Unique, who almost never eats breakfast before 11 a.m., regularly throws this dish together. It's best in the summer months when tomatoes are at their most delicious.

If you like simple, tasty, clean and healthy vegetarian food, there's a good chance you'll love this recipe, which is about as easy to prepare as breakfast can ever be—ideal for sufferers of the Gremlin Boogie.

Milton's method ☞ Toast the bread. Spread the tahini paste liberally over each slice of toast. Arrange the sliced tomatoes on top of the tahini.

Drizzle about one teaspoon of soy sauce, or more to taste, over the tomatoes on each piece of toast.

Scatter the chopped parsley over the toast and serve immediately. Eat this with knives and forks (the tomatoes will quite likely fall off if you try to eat it with your hands!).

O God,

that men should put an enemy in their mouths to steal away their brains! That we should, with joy, pleasance, revel, and applause,

TRANSFORM OURSELVES INTO

BEASTS!

William Shakespeare (*Othello*)

TRADITIONAL JAPANESE BREAKFAST

3½ oz short-grain rice

—

2 tbsp mixed Japanese pickles, such as cucumber, daikon, cabbage

For the "leek and potato" miso soup:

—

1 tbsp instant dashi (Japanese stock) or vegetable stock powder

—

2¼ cups boiling water

—

2 medium-sized potatoes, peeled and chopped into small cubes

—

1 tbsp white miso paste

—

1 spring onion, very finely chopped

DIFFICULTY: ★★★★ TIME: ★★★

This dish might not be to everyone's (westernized) taste on a hungover morning, and it's also a breakfast with many components—rice, grilled fish, miso soup, pickles and a Japanese-style omelette—and some relatively obscure ingredients. Having said that, this is as clean, wholesome and nutritious as breakfast gets, so if anything is going to make you feel better it may well be this. However, I advise you to steer clear of tofu with a hangover (vegetarians: you may shoot me now); I've used cubes of potato instead.

Milton's method ☞ Cook the rice according to the instructions.

For the miso soup: Put the instant dashi stock in a pan with the boiling water. Add the potato and simmer over medium heat for about six minutes, or until the potato is cooked.

Ladle some soup from the pan into a bowl and dissolve the miso in it. Gradually return the miso mixture to the soup. Stir the soup gently but don't let it come to the boil once you've added the miso. Turn off the heat and add the chopped spring onion. Serve hot in small bowls.

For the fish:

1-inch piece of fresh ginger, finely chopped

—

1 spring onion, finely chopped

—

2 tbsp soy sauce

—

2 5-oz fillets of salmon

For the omelette (tamagoyaki):

3 medium free-range eggs

—

1 tsp sugar

—

2 tsp soy sauce

—

1 tsp bonito flakes or instant dashi powder (optional)

—

vegetable oil for cooking

For the fish: Mix the ginger, spring onion and soy sauce together and pour over the salmon fillets. Leave them to stand at room temperature for 15 minutes.

Pour a little boiling water into the grill pan and place the fish on the grill rack above the water (this keeps it moist while it grills). Grill the fish under medium to high heat for about 5–6 minutes on each side, taking care not to overcook it.

For the omelette: Combine the eggs, sugar, soy sauce and bonito flakes (or instant dashi), if using, and mix the ingredients thoroughly.

Heat a little vegetable oil in a small, non-stick frying pan over medium to high heat and add the egg mixture. Agitate the eggs, using a wooden spoon, so the texture of the omelette remains fluffy.

When the eggs are half-cooked, fold the omelette in half, to make a semi-circle, then fold the curving section inwards to form a rectangle, and then fold the ends inwards until you have what looks like a little square package. This creates the distinctive layered effect, called *tamagoyaki*, characteristic of a Japanese omelette.

Flip the "package" over and cook for a further two minutes. Cut into quarters.

To serve: Japanese etiquette decrees that you place the bowl of rice on your left and the bowl of miso soup on your right. Serve the fish on a separate plate, the pickles in a small bowl, and the omelette on another small plate. Now test your hungover skills with chopsticks.

CARROT, ORANGE, APPLE AND GINGER JUICE

1-inch piece of fresh ginger

—

3 medium-sized carrots, peeled

—

3 medium-sized oranges, peeled

—

2 apples, peeled, cored and chopped

DIFFICULTY: ★ TIME: ★

I realize that the idea of any kind of food might be off-putting in the condition you're in, but taking some positive action to try to improve your condition will have an important psychological impact (never, ever underestimate the psychology of hangovers). This very simple and healthy elixir, which includes ginger—a well-known antiemetic that helps prevents nausea and vomiting—could be your first step on the road to recovery. It screams "health" at you—but not so loudly that it hurts, I hope. If you're making this much effort to purify yourself, I suggest you buy wholly organic ingredients.

However, you will need a proper juicer (not a blender) to juice the apples and carrots. If you haven't got one, then it's back to the drawing board (or bed) for you.

Milton's method ☞ Follow your juicer instructions to prepare the fruit and vegetables to ensure they are small enough to squeeze in the juicer's feed tube. Put the ginger in first, and then the other ingredients. After you have juiced the ingredients, pour the juice into glasses and give it a stir to make sure it's well mixed.

The obvious place for you to head is your nearest health-food store, perhaps with your tail between your legs. Maybe you're already a regular. If so, order your usual lentil salad to take home. If you are new to this type of establishment, though, then be wary of TOFU, which is best avoided (whether you're hungover or not). The way to do this is to ask your server in a very loud and clear voice when you are pointing at dishes behind the counter that you are thinking about buying "and does that contain tofu?" If the answer is in the affirmative, then your desire to purchase it should be expressed in the negative.

Well worth the investment in your fragile state, and available at all good health-food stores, are pre-prepared fruit smoothies of the thick and gloopy variety with no water or sugar added. These so readily suggest healthiness that, whatever the actual physical effect on you, they will be of great psychological benefit—never to be underestimated.

MILTON CRAWFORD'S
IDEAL HUNGOVER DAY

Is there such a thing as the ideal hungover day?
Well, I have in mind just such a thing, a day when
a hangover makes impressions more vivid and I
exist in a kind of hazy, tired and dreamy state of
hungover bliss. It's a bit like waking up after
having been shipwrecked the night before and suddenly
realizing that you've landed on a pristine deserted island with a
white sand beach dotted with green coconuts full of cool lemonade.

There are certain preconditions about what this day must be like
that are out of my control. For one, it must be sunny. And it has to
be warm. It's no good having to shiver with a hangover.

After I've pulled back the curtains just far enough to let the warm
sun fall on my face, I head into the kitchen and fix myself a freshly
squeezed Sicilian blood orange and pomegranate juice. I'll down a
cup of its dark-red voluptuous loveliness, then pick up a couple of
limes and grab an ice-cold bottle of sparkling mineral water from
the fridge to make myself a pint of salted lime soda (see page 68) for
the purposes of rehydration. I do not go within a sniff of any
caffeine; I prefer to be relaxed rather than jittery.

I then indulge in a spot of superstition among the bottles strewn
around the living room like jetsam on dawn's hungover beach.
If I was drinking wine the previous night, I'll stick thirteen pins
into a cork to exorcise the evil phenolic spirits that are still haunting
my frontal lobe, in the tradition of Haitian voodoo ceremony.

I'll then start the more practical clean-up of the detritus of the
previous night's bacchanalian binge, picking up the green-glassed
vessels shot through with shafts of morning sunlight that stream
through gaps in the curtain. As I pick up the pieces that lie around
me, it's like reassembling myself.

I head out of the house and cycle through the drowsy warmth of a summer's morning to the beach or, even better, a lake or river. I enjoy a light swim, which ends with floating on my back in the full, hot gaze of the sun.

Greatly refreshed by this gentle exercise, I meet up with a much-loved friend for brunch. What food it is will, of course, depend on the particular type of hangover I have, but favorites include a Swiss rösti with poached eggs and smoked salmon eggs Benedict.

After a good chit-chat and possibly a browse through the papers (or a glance at a book with a fruity vein of misanthropic humor running through it) we might adjourn to the shade of a towering tree in the park, perhaps even with a bottle of something cold, sparkling and alcoholic. Or maybe we'll go for a walk through the countryside and stop for a hearty ploughman's at a pub with a beautiful bucolic beer garden.

And after that… well, who knows? Sometimes, I'm merely happy to be a prisoner in the jail of fate.

So you see, I'm not quite so dissipated as you might have thought: essentially my ideal hungover day is sunshine, light exercise, fresh air, fruit juice and companionship; genuinely the finer things in life (except for the fruit juice, that is).

Acknowledgments

I've come a long way from just a few years ago, when a hungover breakfast meant a smoke and a trip to the boozer. This conversion is largely because of my hungover muse, who shall remain nameless: she knows who she is. It was with her, in Prague, that I shared my favorite, and certainly most peculiar, hungover breakfast. I stumbled out of our rented apartment the morning after a night of Czech pilsner and Polish vodka and bought the breakfast by randomly pointing at things behind a deli counter while the muse waited in bed. I came out of the deli with a whole roast chicken, some roll-mop herrings, a slab of plain chocolate, a loaf of bread and a big box of loose leaf tea and took it back to the apartment, where we ate it all while lying in a hot bath. I only got out of the bath to fetch a bottle of black vodka from the fridge and two glasses to take back to the bathroom with me. Those were the days.

More than anyone else, though, I want to thank Graeme Rodrigo at 300million for thrashing the idea for this book into shape and making it all look so fantastic. Thanks also to the rest of the brilliant, "thrusting" team at 300million, especially Matt Baxter and Katie Morgan, who between them are responsible for the illustrations.

Anna Mayer, Thomas Macken and "Dobber" very kindly provided their recipe for a fantastic Mexican breakfast. Thank you to Jimmy Robertson for the tahini toast recipe, for cooking a recipe or two and being a lab rat (with constructive suggestions) for a couple of the others. Thanks also to Tomomi Kojo-Robertson for helping out with the Japanese breakfast and for sampling some of my cooking, and to Simon Telfer for chowing down on the chorizo omelette.

Thanks to my agent, Andrew Gordon, who has shown his usual skill in helping to arrange a relatively unusual collaboration. Thanks also to my editor Rosemary Davidson and her team at Square Peg and to Jan Bowmer, whose copy-editing skills and food expertise greatly improved a number of the recipes in this book.

The author and the publisher wish to point out that it is you who has gotten yourself drunk. We will not accept any responsibility for either your drunken condition, your hungover state or any implications for your health arising thereof. That being the case, it is also not our responsibility to cure you of your condition, and any accidents or misadventures you may have while attempting to do so yourself are made entirely at your own risk. Good luck!

Please do get drunk responsibly.

The author further wishes to point out that he has thoroughly researched all recipes and, to the best of his abilities, believes the ingredients, quantities and methods to be entirely correct. He will not accept responsibility for failed attempts at cooking that end up looking like a dog's dinner. Good luck (again).

Anna and Tommy's Mexican
    Breakfast, 30
Apples
    Cardamom Porridge with
        Spicy Apple Sauce, 80
    Carrot, Orange, Apple and
        Ginger Juice, 118
Avocado, Potato Hash with, and
    Bacon, 82

Bacon
    Classic Bacon Sandwich, The,
        52
    Elvis Presley Peanut Butter,
        Banana, and Bacon
        Sandwich, The, 47
    English Breakfast Tortilla,
        The, 90
    Potato Hash with Avocado
        and Bacon, 82
    Tagliatelle alla Carbonara, 88
Banana
    Banana and Passion Fruit
        Smoothie, 106
    Elvis Presley Peanut Butter,
        Banana, and Bacon
        Sandwich, The, 47
    French Toast with Banana
        Compote, 96
Bean, Spicy Sausage and,
    Casserole, 86
Berries Compote, Summer, with
    Greek Yogurt and Granola,
    70

Beverages
    Bloody Mary, 40
    Carrot, Orange, Apple and
        Ginger Juice, 118
    Lemon Lassi, 67
    Lime Soda, 68
    Sweet Lassi, 100
    Virgin Piña Colada, 66
Bloody Mary, 40
Boiled Eggs with Potato Farl
    Fingers, 58
Breakfast Burger, The, 78

Cardamom Porridge with Spicy
    Apple Sauce, 80
Carrot, Orange, Apple and
    Ginger Juice, 118
Cheat's Smoked Salmon Eggs
    Benedict, 112
Cheese
    Cheese, Red Onion and
        Chutney Toasties, 84
    Leek, Cheese and Mustard
        Mash with Sausages and
        Onion Gravy, 50
    Melon, Feta, Mint and Ham
        Salad, 111
    Scrambled Eggs with
        Caramelized Onion and
        Feta Cheese, 48
    Stilton and Pears on Toast, 24
Chorizo Omelette, 77
Classic Bacon Sandwich, The,
    52

Croissants, Nutella and Hot
   Chocolate, 56

Desserts
   Banana and Passion Fruit
      Smoothie, 106
   Ice Cream Smoothie, 55
   Knickerbocker Glory with
      Refreshers, The, 72
Deviled Kidneys on Toast,
   36

Eggs
   Anna and Tommy's Mexican
      Breakfast, 30
   Boiled Eggs with Potato Farl
      Fingers, 58
   Cheat's Smoked Salmon
      Eggs Benedict, 112
   Chorizo Omelette, 77
   Eggs Bhurji with Fried
      Bread, 29
   English Breakfast Tortilla,
      The, 90
   Huevos Rancheros, 42
   Kedgeree, 38
   Scrambled Eggs with
      Caramelized Onion and
      Feta Cheese, 48
   Shakshuka, 34
   Swiss Rösti and Poached
      Eggs, 104
   Traditional Japanese
      Breakfast, 116

Turkish Breakfast, A, 95
Elvis Presley Peanut Butter,
   Banana and Bacon
   Sandwich, The, 47
English Breakfast Tortilla, The,
   90

Fish Finger Sandwich, Milton
   Crawford's, (with Garlic
   Green Pea Mayo), 98
French Toast with Banana
   Compote, 96

Garlic Green Pea Mayo,
   Milton Crawford's Fish
   Finger Sandwich with,
   98
Granola, Summer Berries
   Compote with Greek
   Yogurt and, 70

Ham, Melon, Feta, Mint and
   Salad, 111
Hot Chocolate, Croissants,
   Nutella and, 56
Huevos Rancheros, 42

Ice Cream Smoothie, 55

Kedgeree, 38
Kidneys, Deviled, on Toast,
   36
Knickerbocker Glory with
   Refreshers, The, 72

Lassi
  Lemon Lassi, 67
  Sweet Lassi, 100
Leek, Cheese and Mustard
  Mash with Sausages and
  Onion Gravy, 50
Lemon and Demerara Sugar
  Pancakes, 64
Lemon Lassi, 67
Lime Soda, 68

Melon, Feta, Mint and Ham
  Salad, 111
Milton Crawford's Fish Finger
  Sandwich (with Garlic
  Green Pea Mayo), 98

Nutella, Croissants, Hot
  Chocolate, and 56

Omelette, Chorizo, 77
Onion, Caramelized, Scrambled
  Eggs with, and Feta
  Cheese, 48
Onion, Red, and Cheese and
  Chutney Toasties, 84
Onion Gravy, Leek, Cheese
  and Mustard Mash with
  Sausages and, 50

Pancakes, Lemon and Demerara
  Sugar, 64
Passion Fruit and Banana
  Smoothie, 106

Peanut Butter, Elvis Presley,
  Banana and Bacon
  Sandwich, The, 47
Pears, Stilton and, on Toast, 24
Perfect Tea and Toast, The,
  102
Pizza with Yesterday's Roast, 32
Porridge, Cardamom, with
  Spicy Apple Sauce, 80
Potatoes
  Boiled Eggs with Potato Farl
    Fingers, 58
  Leek, Cheese and Mustard
    Mash with Sausages and
    Onion Gravy, 50
  Potato Hash with Avocado
    and Bacon, 82
  Swiss Rösti and Poached
    Eggs, 104
  Traditional Japanese
    Breakfast, 116

Sandwiches
  Breakfast Burger, The, 78
  Cheese, Red Onion and
    Chutney Toasties, 84
  Classic Bacon Sandwich, The,
    52
  Milton Crawford's Fish
    Finger Sandwich (with
    Garlic Green Pea Mayo), 98
  Peanut Butter, Elvis Presley,
    Banana and Bacon
    Sandwich, The, 47

Sausage
  Anna and Tommy's Mexican
    Breakfast, 30
  Breakfast Burger, The, 78
  Chorizo Omelette, 77
  English Breakfast Tortilla,
    The, 90
  Leek, Cheese and Mustard
    Mash with Sausages and
    Onion Gravy, 50
  Spicy Sausage and Bean
    Casserole, 86
Scrambled Eggs with
    Caramelized Onion and
    Feta Cheese, 48
Seafood
  Cheat's Smoked Salmon Eggs
    Benedict, 112
  Kedgeree, 38
  Milton Crawford's Fish
    Finger Sandwich (with
    Garlic Green Pea Mayo), 98
  Traditional Japanese
    Breakfast, 116
Shakshuka, 34
Smoked Salmon, Cheat's, Eggs
    Benedict, 112

Smoothies
  Banana and Passion Fruit
    Smoothie, 106
  Ice Cream Smoothie, 55
Stilton and Pears on Toast, 24
Spicy Sausage and Bean
    Casserole, 86
Summer Berries Compote with
    Greek Yogurt and Granola,
    70
Sweet Lassi, 100
Swiss Rösti and Poached Eggs,
    104

Tagliatelle alla Carbonara, 88
Tahini and Tomato Toast, 114
Traditional Japanese Breakfast,
    116
Turkish Breakfast, A, 95

Virgin Piña Colada, 66

Yogurt, Greek, and Summer
    Berries Compote, with
    Granola, 70

Amateur chef, professional boozer, poet, traveler and essayist, Milton Crawford is also a fantastic drinker. He describes drinking as his one true talent in life. He states that "seven days without a drink makes one weak." He once said that a hangover is like being crucified—it offers ordinary mortals the chance of resurrection on a daily basis.

His politics are libertarian (to say the least).

His heroes are people who found the palace of wisdom via the road of excess, to paraphrase William Blake. They include Tolstoy and Buddha. His ambition is to survive for long enough to become a similarly wise man in his old age as these two grand ex-debauchees.

When he's not drunk, Milton reads, writes, cooks, travels and swims. He has a cat and occasionally lives in London because it's "good for his career."

Find out what Milton's doing now on Twitter:
Twitter.com/MiltonCrawford